Pocket TOKYO

TOP SIGHTS • LOCAL LIFE • MADE EASY

Rebecca Milner

In This Book

QuickStart Guide

Your keys to understanding the city – we help you decide what to do and how to do it

Need to Know
Tips for a smooth trip

Neighbourhoods
What's where

Explore Tokyo

The best things to see and do, neighbourhood by neighbourhood

Top Sights
Make the most of your visit

Local Life
The insider's city

The Best of Tokyo

The city's highlights in handy lists to help you plan

Best Walks
See the city on foot

Tokyo's Best...
The best experiences

Survival Guide

Tips and tricks for a seamless, hassle-free city experience

Getting Around
Travel like a local

Essential Information
Including where to stay

Our selection of the city's best places to eat, drink and experience:

⊙ **Sights**

✖ **Eating**

☺ **Drinking**

★ **Entertainment**

🔒 **Shopping**

These symbols give you the vital information for each listing:

- ☏ Telephone Numbers
- ⊙ Opening Hours
- ℗ Parking
- ⊝ Nonsmoking
- @ Internet Access
- 🛜 Wi-Fi Access
- 🌱 Vegetarian Selection
- 📖 English-Language Menu
- 👪 Family-Friendly
- 🐾 Pet-Friendly
- 🚌 Bus
- ⛴ Ferry
- Ⓜ Metro
- Ⓢ Subway
- 🚊 Tram
- 🚆 Train

Find each listing quickly on maps for each neighbourhood:

Bar Hemingway

16 ⊙ Map p233, B2

Legend has it that Hemi̲
self, wielding a machine
rate this timber-pan
ered bar during
showpiece is a
en by Papa ar
town. Dress
s.com; Hôtel Rit
⊙6.30pm-2a

6 ⊙ *Plac*

QuickStart Guide 7

Explore Tokyo 21

Worth a Trip:

The Best of Tokyo **149**

Tokyo's Best Walks

Tokyo's Best ...

Survival Guide **173**

ラオケ&パーティ747
5F
漢方エステ
タンポポ
年中無休 24時間営業
新宿国際劇場
3F
台湾料理
味王
小酒館
TEL (3352)9534
三平酒寮
1F
2F
B1
4F
Green Peas

QuickStart Guide

Welcome to Tokyo

Tokyo is a city forever reaching into the future, resulting in sci-fi streetscapes of crackling neon and soaring towers. Yet it is also a city steeped in history, where you can find traces of the shogun's capital on the kabuki stage or under the cherry blossoms. It's a tapestry of sensorial madness unlike anywhere else in the world.

Shinjuku (p96)
MARC FERNANDEZ DIAZ/GETTY IMAGES ©

Tokyo
Top Sights

Tsukiji Market (p34)

The world's largest fish market is Tokyo's most unique sight, and a rare peek into the workings of the city. It's only around in its current form for a limited time too: the market moves in November 2016.

PAUL DYMOND/GETTY IMAGES ©

Sumo in Ryōgoku (p44)

Salt-slinging, belly-slapping and solemn ritual are all part of the spectacle that is sumo, Japan's ancient, traditional sport. Catch a tournament at the national stadium in Ryōgoku, or a morning practice session.

Meiji-jingū (p84)

Tokyo's most famous Shintō shrine is shrouded in woods. It's a peaceful haven that feels worlds away from the city, even though it is right in the thick of it.

Sensō-ji (p134)

The spiritual home of Tokyoites' ancestors, Sensō-ji was founded more than 1000 years before Tokyo got its start. Today the temple retains an alluring, lively atmosphere redolent of Edo (old Tokyo under the shogun).

Kabuki (p36)

Kabuki, a form of stylised, traditional Japanese theatre, features stories based on popular legend and an all-male cast in dramatic make-up and decadent costumes. Catch a performance at Kabuki-za, Tokyo's newly rebuilt kabuki theatre.

Roppongi Hills (p48)

This is no ordinary mall: it's a utopian microcity with a world-class art museum. Love it or hate it, Roppongi Hills is integral to understanding the Tokyo of today, and possibly the Tokyo of tomorrow.

Tokyo National Museum (p122)

Japan's premier museum houses the world's largest collection of Japanese art and antiquities, such as swords, gilded screens, kimonos and colourful *ukiyo-e* (woodblock prints).

Mt Fuji (p146)

Japan's national symbol is a perfect, snowcapped cone. On a clear day, you can catch a glimpse from atop a Tokyo skyscraper, but nothing compares to the thrill of seeing a sunrise from the summit.

Imperial Palace & Garden (p22)

Take a tour of the leafy grounds of the imperial family's residence, or content yourself to stroll along the ancient moat and climb an old castle keep in the garden.

Ōedo Onsen Monogatari (p144)

Bubbling hot springs piped in from below Tokyo Bay fill the baths at Ōedo Onsen Monogatari, a combination of public bathhouse and theme park that is Japanese to the core.

Ghibli Museum (p108)

Even those uninitiated in the magical world of master animator Miyazaki Hayao (*Princess Mononoke, Spirited Away*) will find this museum dedicated to him and his works enchanting. Fans won't want to leave.

Tokyo Local Life

Insider tips to help you find the real city

Get beyond the big-ticket sights and see Tokyo from a local's point of view. Explore the city's bohemian enclaves and historical quarters, its fascinating subcultures, quirky shops, hip cafes and sublime nightlife.

Shopping in Daikanyama & Naka-Meguro (p62)

▶ Fashionable boutiques
▶ Riverside cafes

These twin districts feel light years away from hectic Shibuya, just minutes away. Daikanyama has shops from up-and-coming Japanese designers; Naka-Meguro has a leafy canal flanked by restaurants and cafes.

Hanging Out in Shimo-Kitazawa (p80)

▶ Bohemian culture
▶ Bars and pubs

Shimo-Kitazawa, with its colourful street scene and down-to-earth vibe, has been a bastion of counter-culture for decades. Come for the secondhand stores, coffee shops, raucous *izakaya* (Japanese-style pubs) and hole-in-the-wall bars.

East Shinjuku at Night (p98)

▶ Colourful nightlife
▶ Late-night eats

Walk through the crackling neon canyons of Tokyo's largest nightlife district, piled high with bars, cabarets and karaoke parlours, then raise a glass (and slurp some noodles) in one of the wooden shanties that make up Golden Gai.

An Afternoon in Akihabara (p118)

▶ Pop culture
▶ Quirky shops and cafes

Akihabara, epicentre of Tokyo's *otaku* (geek) subculture, is an alternative universe of maid cafes (where the waitresses dress like French maids) and *rāmen* (soup and noodles with meat and vegetables) vending machines, anime collectables and vintage video arcades.

A Stroll Through Historic Yanaka (p124)

▶ Art galleries
▶ Hidden lanes

The rare neighbourhood to survive both the Great Kantō Earthquake and the firebombing of WWII, Yanaka looks and feels like the Tokyo of 100 years ago. It's long been a favourite of local artists.

Bowls of ramen noodles at a Shinjuku cafe

Meguro-gawa (p63)

Other great places to experience the city like a local:

Ura-Hara (p94)

Ebisu-yokochō (p67)

Weekend markets in Harajuku (p91)

Nishi-Azabu (p91)

Naka-dōri (p30)

Book Town Jimbōchō (p116)

Meguro Interior Shops Community (p68)

Nonbei-yokochō (p77)

Namiki-dōri (p41)

Nezu no Taiyaki (p130)

Tokyo
Day Planner

Day One

Start the day in Harajuku with a visit to **Meiji-jingū** (p84), Tokyo's signature Shintō shrine. Next stroll down **Takeshita-dōri** (p88), the famous teen-fashion bazaar. Work (and shop) your way through the back streets of Harajuku, and then head to **Omote-sandō** (p88) to see the jaw-dropping contemporary architecture along this stylish boulevard. Break for lunch at local fave **Harajuku Gyōza-rō** (p91).

Head down to Shibuya (you can walk) and continue your schooling in Tokyo pop culture by wandering the lanes of this youthful neighbourhood. Don't miss **Shibuya Center-gai** (p74), the main drag, and the mural, **Myth of Tomorrow** (p74), in the train station. Stick around Shibuya until dusk to see **Shibuya Crossing** (p74) all lit up.

Take the train to Shinjuku and immerse yourself in the swarming crowds and neon lights of this notorious nightlife district. The **Tokyo Metropolitan Government Offices** (p101) observatories stay open until 10pm, for free night views. From around 9pm the shanty bars of **Golden Gai** (p99) come to life; take your pick from the quirky offerings and finish up with a time-honoured Tokyo tradition: a late-night bowl of noodles at **Nagi** (p99).

Day Two

Skip breakfast and head directly to **Tsukiji Market** (p34), spending the morning exploring the cobblestone lanes of the inner market and the bustling stalls of the outer market. You'll have to get there by 4am to get a spot at the tuna auction; otherwise, the inner market opens to the public from 9am. Have lunch at **Daiwa Sushi** (p40).

From Tsukiji, it's an easy walk to the landscaped garden **Hama-rikyū Onshi-teien** (p39), where you can stop for tea in the garden's teahouse. Then take a **Tokyo Cruise** (p177) river boat up to Asakusa, to see the temple complex **Sensō-ji** (p134), the shrine **Asakusa-jinja** (p137) and the maze of old-world alleys that surround these sights. There are lots of shops selling traditional crafts and foodstuffs around here too. Don't miss the temple complex all lit up from dusk. For dinner, dig into the cuisine of old Edo at **Komagata Dojō** (p139).

Head up nearby **Tokyo Sky Tree** (p137) for the night view to end all night views. Or instead, get a view of the illuminated tower and the snaking Sumida-gawa (and a beer) from the **Asahi Sky Room** (p142).

Short on time?
We've arranged Tokyo's must-sees into these day-by-day itineraries to make sure you see the very best of the city in the time you have available.

Day Three

☀ Spend the morning exploring the many attractions of **Ueno-kōen** (p127), Tokyo's traditional cultural centre. There are museums, like the top-notch **Tokyo National Museum** (p122), plus centuries-old temples and shrines, like **Kiyōmizu Kannon-dō** (p127) and **Ueno Tōshō-gū** (p127), and **Ueno Zoo** (p129). Have lunch at historic **Hantei** (p129).

☀ Spend a peaceful afternoon exploring the narrow lanes of neighbouring Yanaka, a long-time favourite with local artists. Don't miss the nostalgic shopping street **Yanaka Ginza** (p124), the charming **Asakura Chōso Museum** (p125) and the hip gallery **SCAI the Bathhouse** (p125). Along the way you'll also see many small temples, tiny craft shops and more galleries.

☾ At dusk, head back to Ueno and take a stroll through the old-fashioned, open-air market, **Ameya-yokochō** (p127). Then go for dinner at **Shinsuke** (p129), a fantastic *izakaya* (Japanese-style pub). If your accommodation is on the west side of town, stop off in Ebisu to check out the lively bar scene, starting with **Buri** (p68). Otherwise, have another round of Shinsuke's excellent sake, or go for a nightcap at bookstore-slash-bar **Bousingot** (p131).

Day Four

☀ Make a pilgrimage to the western outskirts of the city to visit the **Ghibli Museum** (p109) – and enter the world of Japan's most beloved animator, Miyazaki Hayao. After the museum, walk back through **Inokashira-kōen** (p109) to Kichijōji Station. Alternatively, you could spend this morning relaxing in the tubs at 'onsen theme park' **Ōedo Onsen Monogatari** (p145) on Tokyo Bay.

☀ Head to one of Tokyo's offbeat neighbourhoods to see another side of the city. You could continue your pop-culture education with a walk through the anime-mad district of **Aki-habara** (p118), hang with a boho crowd in **Shimo-Kitazawa** (p80) or do some shopping in the fashionable residential enclaves of **Daikanyama** and **Naka-Meguro** (p62).

☾ Now back into the thick of things. Check out **Roppongi Hills** (p48), the first of Tokyo's new breed of live-work-and-play megamalls in Roppongi. On the top floor of a tower here is the excellent **Mori Art Museum** (p49), which stays open until 10pm. Get dinner at lively *izakaya*-like **Jōmon** (p55), then head out into the wilds of Roppongi's infamous nightlife. Be sure to get in a round of karaoke.

Need to Know

For more information, see Survival Guide (p173)

Currency
Japanese yen (¥)

Language
Japanese

Visas
Citizens of 61 countries, including Australia, Canada, Hong Kong, Korea, New Zealand, Singapore, UK, USA and almost all European nations do not require visas to enter Japan for stays of 90 days or fewer.

Money
Post offices and some convenience stores have international ATMs. Credit cards are accepted at major establishments, though it's best to have cash on hand.

Mobile Phones
Local SIM cards cannot be used in overseas phones and only 3G phones will work in Japan; rental phones are available.

Time
Japan Standard Time (GMT plus nine hours)

Plugs & Adaptors
Plugs have two flat pins; electrical current is 100V. North American appliances will work; others will require an adaptor.

Tipping
Tipping is not common practice in Japan, though top-end restaurants will add a 10% service charge to your bill.

❶ Before You Go

Your Daily Budget

Budget less than ¥8000
▶ Dorm bed ¥2800
▶ Bowl of noodles ¥800
▶ Free sights and cheaper museums
▶ One-act tickets for kabuki ¥1500

Midrange ¥8000–¥20,000
▶ Double room in a business hotel ¥12,000
▶ Dinner for two at an *izakaya* (Japanese-style pub) ¥6000
▶ Mezzanine seats for kabuki ¥5000

Top End more than ¥20,000
▶ Double room in a four-star hotel ¥35,000
▶ Dinner for two at a top sushi restaurant ¥35,000
▶ Top seats for kabuki ¥20,000

Useful Websites

Lonely Planet (www.lonelyplanet.com/tokyo) Destination information, hotel bookings, traveller forum and more.

Go Tokyo (www.gotokyo.org/en/index.html) Tokyo's official site covers sights, events and tours.

Time Out Tokyo (www.timeout.jp) Arts and entertainment listings.

Advance Planning

One month before Book tickets online for kabuki, sumo and the Imperial Palace tour; make reservations at top-end restaurants; book your hotel now and you may lock in a better rate.

One week before Scan web listings for festivals, live-music shows and exhibitions.

② Arriving in Tokyo

Narita Airport is 66km east of Tokyo; the more convenient Haneda Airport is on the city's southern edge. However, some flights to Haneda arrive in the middle of the night when a taxi (budget around ¥6000) is your only option.

✈ From Narita Airport

Destination	Best Transport
Asakusa	Keisei Skyliner to Ueno, then subway (Ginza line)
Ginza, Roppongi, Ebisu	Keisei Skyliner to Ueno, then subway (Hibiya line)
Marunouchi (Tokyo Station), Shinjuku, Shibuya	Narita Express
Ueno	Keisei Skyliner

✈ From Haneda Airport

Destination	Best Transport
Ginza, Asakusa	Keikyū line to Sengakuji, then subway (Asakusa line)
Ebisu, Shibuya, Shinjuku	Keikyū line to Shinagawa, then JR Yamanote line
Marunouchi (Tokyo Station), Ueno	Tokyo Monorail to Hamamatsuchō, then JR Yamanote line
Roppongi	Tokyo Monorail to Hamamatsuchō, then subway (Ōedo line from Daimon Station)

🚇 From Tokyo Train Station

Tokyo Station, the *shinkansen* (bullet train) terminus, is serviced by the JR Yamanote line and the Marunouchi subway line. There are taxi ranks in front of both the Marunouchi Central and Yaesu Central exits.

③ Getting Around

Tokyo's public-transport system – a tourist attraction in its own right – is excellent. It's a good idea to get a prepaid Suica or Pasmo pass (they're interchangeable). These work on all trains and subways and mean you won't have to worry about purchasing paper tickets.

🚇 Train

The rail network, which includes 13 subway lines (run by either Tokyo Metro or Toei) and Japan Rail (JR) lines, will take you pretty much anywhere you need to go. It's the quickest and easiest way to get around, though it doesn't run between midnight and 5am. With a Suica or Pasmo pass you can transfer seamlessly between lines. All train stations have English signage and the lines are conveniently colour-coded. The most useful line is the JR Yamanote line, an elevated loop line that runs through many key sightseeing areas.

🚗 Taxi

Taxis only make economic sense if you've got a group of four; additionally, taxi drivers rarely speak English and know only major destinations. Still, they're your only option after midnight.

🚲 Bicycle

Bicycles are good for getting around quieter neighbourhoods where traffic is thinner; some guesthouses have bicycles to lend.

Boat

Tourist boats run up and down the Sumida-gawa; they're not cheap or efficient, but the views are lovely.

Tokyo
Neighbourhoods

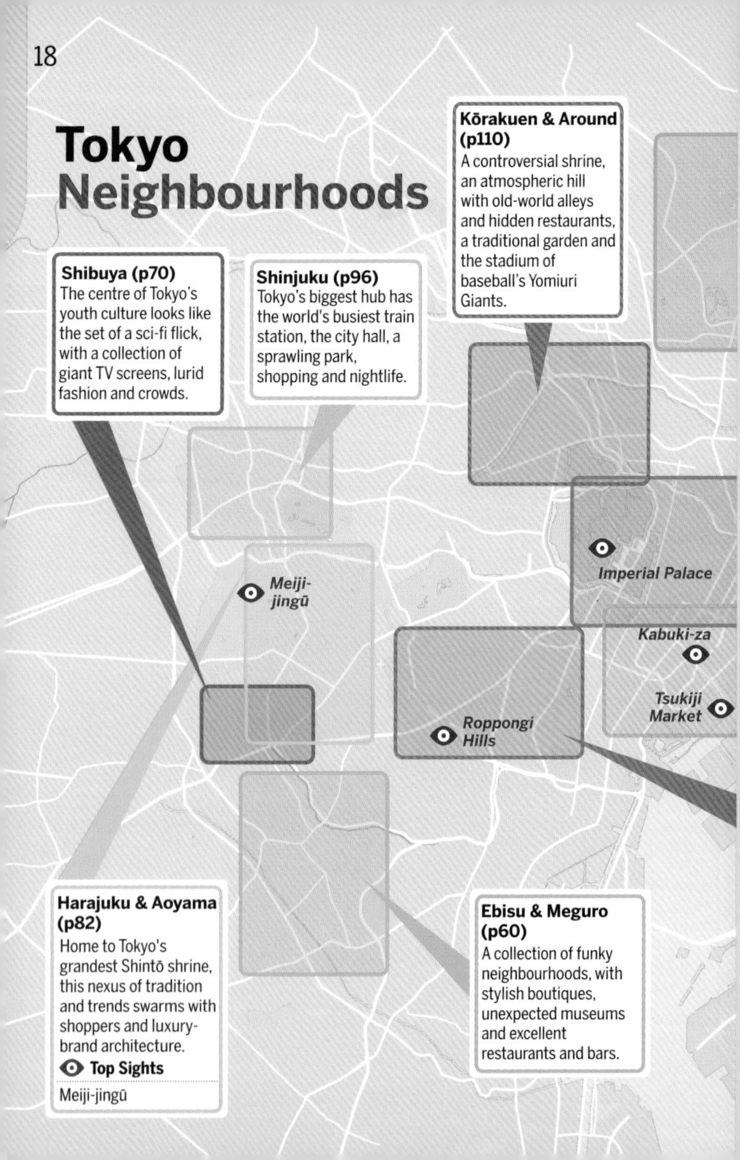

Kōrakuen & Around (p110)
A controversial shrine, an atmospheric hill with old-world alleys and hidden restaurants, a traditional garden and the stadium of baseball's Yomiuri Giants.

Shibuya (p70)
The centre of Tokyo's youth culture looks like the set of a sci-fi flick, with a collection of giant TV screens, lurid fashion and crowds.

Shinjuku (p96)
Tokyo's biggest hub has the world's busiest train station, the city hall, a sprawling park, shopping and nightlife.

◉ Meiji-jingū

◉ Imperial Palace

◉ Kabuki-za

◉ Tsukiji Market

◉ Roppongi Hills

Harajuku & Aoyama (p82)
Home to Tokyo's grandest Shintō shrine, this nexus of tradition and trends swarms with shoppers and luxury-brand architecture.
◉ **Top Sights**
Meiji-jingū

Ebisu & Meguro (p60)
A collection of funky neighbourhoods, with stylish boutiques, unexpected museums and excellent restaurants and bars.

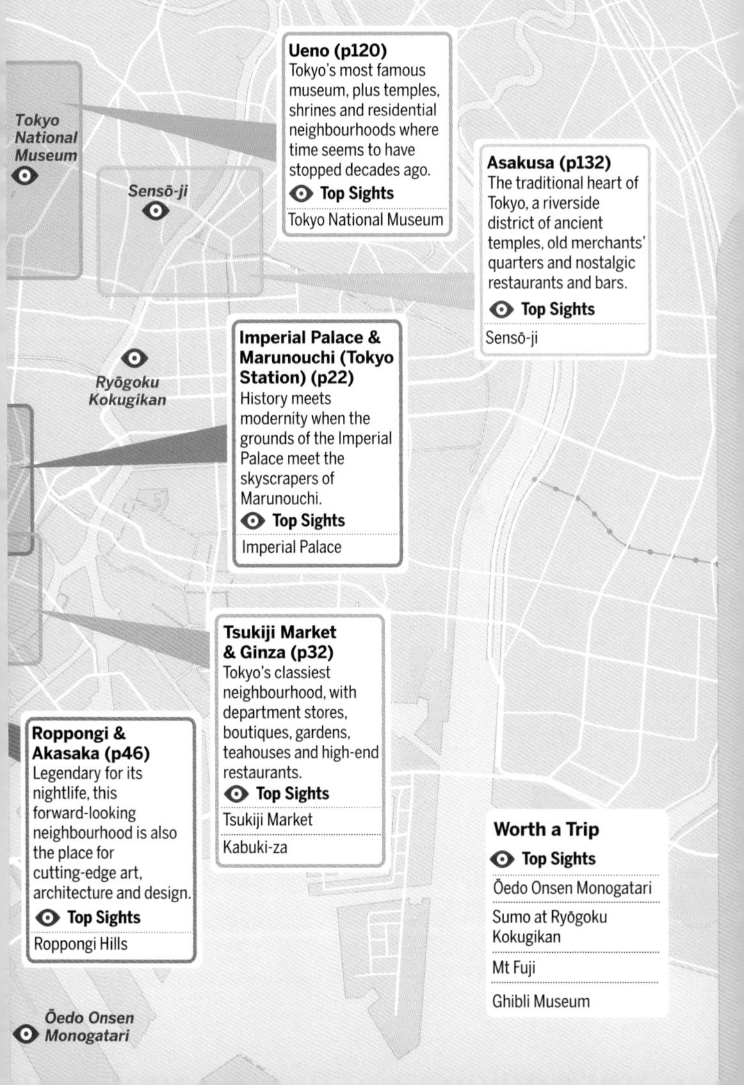

Tokyo National Museum ⊙

Sensō-ji ⊙

Ryōgoku Kokugikan ⊙

Ōedo Onsen Monogatari ⊙

Ueno (p120)
Tokyo's most famous museum, plus temples, shrines and residential neighbourhoods where time seems to have stopped decades ago.

⊙ **Top Sights**

Tokyo National Museum

Asakusa (p132)
The traditional heart of Tokyo, a riverside district of ancient temples, old merchants' quarters and nostalgic restaurants and bars.

⊙ **Top Sights**

Sensō-ji

Imperial Palace & Marunouchi (Tokyo Station) (p22)
History meets modernity when the grounds of the Imperial Palace meet the skyscrapers of Marunouchi.

⊙ **Top Sights**

Imperial Palace

Tsukiji Market & Ginza (p32)
Tokyo's classiest neighbourhood, with department stores, boutiques, gardens, teahouses and high-end restaurants.

⊙ **Top Sights**

Tsukiji Market

Kabuki-za

Roppongi & Akasaka (p46)
Legendary for its nightlife, this forward-looking neighbourhood is also the place for cutting-edge art, architecture and design.

⊙ **Top Sights**

Roppongi Hills

Worth a Trip
⊙ **Top Sights**

Ōedo Onsen Monogatari

Sumo at Ryōgoku Kokugikan

Mt Fuji

Ghibli Museum

Explore
Tokyo

Worth a Trip

Shibuya Crossing (p74)
TOMML/GETTY IMAGES ©

Explore

Imperial Palace & Marunouchi (Tokyo Station)

The Imperial Palace is Tokyo's symbolic centre. The palace grounds include the now public park, Kitanomaru-kōen, home to museums. Nearby Marunouchi is a high-powered business district with dozens of glossy skyscrapers on show. It's establishment Tokyo at its finest, with museums and architectural masterpieces, but also restaurants, bars and shops for the office workers who hold it all together.

Conversely inappropriate.

WIBOWO RUSLI/GETTY IMAGES ©

The Sights in a Day

☼ Take the train to **Tokyo Station** (p27) to see the recently restored 100-year-old building, then head to the **Imperial Palace** (p24). A tour of the grounds begins at 10am (you'll need to book ahead), after which you can spend an hour exploring the **Imperial Palace East Garden** (p25). Grab a light lunch at **Rose Bakery** (p29) or a belly-warming bowl of noodles at **Tokyo Rāmen Street** (p29).

☼ In the afternoon check out some of the excellent museums: the **Intermediateque** (p27) in the new Japan Post Tower or the **National Museum of Modern Art** (p27) and the **Crafts Gallery** (p28), both in Kitanomaru-kōen. Architecture fans will want to see the **Tokyo International Forum** (p27). Alternatively, head over to Nihombashi to see the neighbourhood's namesake, the historic bridge **Nihombashi** (p28), and also to check out the shopping at venerable **Takashimaya** (p30) and the new **Coredo Muromachi** (p30).

★ For dinner, go for classic Japanese at **Hōnen Manpuku** (p29) in Nihombashi. This area gets pretty quiet at night, but there's always a crowd at **So Tired** (p30), which has views of Tokyo Station from its terrace.

Top Sights

Best of Tokyo

Getting There

🚃 **Train** The JR Yamanote line stops at Tokyo Station and Yūrakuchō. Tokyo Station is also serviced by Narita Express and *shinkansen* (bullet train).

Ⓢ **Subway** The Marunouchi line runs through Tokyo Station. Several lines such as Marunouchi, Hanzōmon and Chiyoda lines stop at Ōtemachi; Chiyoda line continues to Nijūbashimae. The Ginza line services Nihombashi and Mitsukoshimae. For Takebashi, take the Tōzai line.

Top Sights
Imperial Palace

The verdant grounds of Japan's Imperial Palace occupy the site of the original Edo-jō, the Tokugawa shogunate's castle when they ruled the land. In its heyday this was the largest fortress in the world, though little remains of it today apart from the moat and stone walls – parts of which you can view up close in the Imperial Palace East Garden. The present palace, completed in 1968, replaced the one built in 1888, which was largely destroyed during WWII.

皇居, Kōkyo

⊙ Map p26, A2

☎ 3213-1111

http://sankan.kunaicho.go.jp/english/index.html

Chiyoda, Chiyoda-ku

admission free

Ⓢ Chiyoda line to Ōtemachi, exits C13b & C10

Imperial Palace East Garden

Don't Miss

Palace Grounds

As it's the home of Japan's emperor and some of the imperial family, the palace buildings are all off limits. It is possible, however, to take a free tour (lasting around 1¼ hours) of a small part of the surrounding grounds, but you must book ahead through the palace website.

Nijū-bashi & the Palace Moat

The original moat, dating to the time of Edo-jō, still wraps around the palace grounds. Even if you skip the tour, you can walk along the edge of the moat to see **Nijū-bashi**, one of Japan's most famous bridges, an elegant succession of stone arches used for formal ceremonies and receptions.

Fujimi-yagura

Behind the bridges rises the Edo-era Fushimi-yagura (伏見櫓) watchtower, which was supposedly relocated from Kyoto in the 17th century. If you take the tour, you'll also get a close-up view of the 1659 watchtower Fujimi-yagura (富士見櫓; Mt Fuji Keep), one of the few remaining original structures.

Imperial Palace East Garden

The **Imperial Palace East Garden** (東御苑; Kōkyo Higashi-gyoen; ☉9am-4pm Nov-Feb, to 4.30pm Mar–mid-Apr, Sep & Oct, to 5pm mid-Apr–Aug, closed Mon & Fri year-round) is open to the public without a reservation. You can see the massive stones used to build the castle walls and can climb on the ruins of one of the keeps. The entrance is via the gate Ōte-mon (大手門); take a token on arrival and return it at the end of your visit.

☑ **Top Tips**

▶ Tours, leaving from the Kikyō-mon gate, run twice daily from Monday to Friday (10am and 1.30pm), but only in the mornings from late July until the end of August. You must sign up in advance through the palace's website. Remember to bring your passport and to pick up the free English audio headset for the tour.

▶ The Imperial Palace East Garden is closed on Mondays and Fridays, so it's easier to book a tour on those days, but it means missing the garden.

✗ **Take a Break**

Not far from Nijū-bashi, Rose Bakery (p29) does light lunches, coffee and cake.

Wind down the day with a drink on the terrace at So Tired (p30), a couple of blocks from Ōte-mon.

Shuto Expwy No 1

E

NIHOMBASHI-MUROMACHI

13

Mitsukoshimae 7

Nihombashi (Nihombashi) 6

Nihombashi

NIHOMBASHI

Showa-dōri

Hatchōbori

HATCHŌBORI

Chūō-dōri

Shin-nihombashi

Mitsukoshimae

Nihombashi-gawa

Nihombashi

12

KYŌBASHI

Yaesu-dōri

CHŪŌ-KU

Takarachō

D

Shuto Expwy No 5

Ōtemachi

Sakura-dōri

YAESU

Chūō-dōri

Kyōbashi

Sakura-dōri

Ginza-itchōme

400 m

0.2 miles

CHIYODA-KU

Ōtemachi

Eitai-dōri

Sotobori-dōri

15

2

JR East Travel Service Center

Tokyo Tokyo Station 8

Kajibashi-dōri

GINZA

Ginza

ŌTEMACHI

Uchibori-dōri

Ote Moat

Oté-mon

Wadakura Sq

Naka-dōri

Intermediateque

Tokyo

10

Tokyo Central Post Office

MARUNOUCHI

10

Tokyo International Forum

Yūrakuchō

14

11

Uchibori-dōri

Babasaki-Moat

9

JNTO Tourist Information Center

YŪRAKUCHŌ

Yūrakuchō

National Museum of Modern Art (MOMAT) 3

Kōkyo Higashi-Gyoen (Imperial Palace East Garden)

Fujimi-yagura

Kikyo-mon

Nijūbashimae

Imperial Palace Outer Garden

Imperial Palace Plaza

Sakuradamon

Hibiya

Harumi-dōri

Hibiya-kōen

Hibiya

Hibiya-dōri

Area not open to public

Imperial Household Agency

Shimo-dōkan Moat

Imperial Palace

Nijū-bashi Megane-bashi

Fukiage Imperial Gardens

Fushimi-yagura

Kōkkai-gijidōmae

Crafts Gallery 5

For reviews see	
◉ Top Sights	p24
◎ Sights	p27
⊗ Eating	p29
◐ Drinking	p30
◐ Shopping	p30

A   B   C   D   E

1   2   3   4

Sights

Intermediateque
MUSEUM

1 Map p26, C3

Dedicated to interdisciplinary experimentation, Intermediateque cherrypicks from the vast collection of the University of Tokyo (Tōdai) to craft a fascinating and wholly contemporary museum experience. Go from viewing the best ornithological taxidermy collection in Japan to a giant pop-art print or the beautifully encased skeleton of a dinosaur. A handsome Tōdai lecture hall is reconstituted as a forum for events, including the playing of 1920s jazz recordings on a gramophone or old movie screenings. (📞5777-8600; www.intermediatheque.jp; 2nd & 3rd fl, JP Tower, 2-7-2 Marunouchi, Chiyoda-ku; admission free; ⏱11am-6pm Tue, Wed, Sat & Sun, to 8pm Thu & Fri; 🚉JR Yamanote line to Tokyo, Marunouchi exit)

Tokyo Station
LANDMARK

2 Map p26, D3

Following a major renovation completed in time for its centenary in 2014, Tokyo Station is in grand form. Kingo Tatsuno's elegant brick building on the Marunouchi side has been expertly restored to include domes faithful to the original design, decorated inside with relief sculptures. (東京駅; www.tokyostationcity.com/en; 1-9 Marunouchi, Chiyoda-ku; 🚉JR lines to Tokyo Station)

National Museum of Modern Art (MOMAT)
MUSEUM

3 Map p26, B1

This collection of over 9000 works is one of the country's best. All pieces date from the Meiji period onwards and impart a sense of a more modern Japan through portraits, photography and contemporary sculptures and video works. There's a wonderful view from the museum towards the Imperial Palace East Garden. (国立近代美術館, Kokuritsu Kindai Bijutsukan; 📞5777-8600; www.momat.go.jp/english; 3-1 Kitanomaru-kōen, Chiyoda-ku; adult/student ¥420/130, extra for special exhibitions; ⏱10am-5pm Tue-Thu, Sat & Sun, to 8pm Fri; 🚇Tōzai line to Takebashi, exit 1b)

Tokyo International Forum
ARCHITECTURE

4 Map p26, C4

This architectural marvel designed by Rafael Viñoly houses a convention and arts centre, with seven auditoriums and a spacious courtyard in which concerts and events are held. The eastern wing looks like a glass ship plying the urban waters; take the lift to the 7th floor and look down on the tiny people below. Visit for the twice-monthly **Ōedo Antique Market** (⏱9am-4pm 1st & 3rd Sun of month) and the daily food trucks serving bargain meals and drinks to local office workers. **Tokyo Station Hotel** (東京ステーションホテル; 📞5220-1112; www.tokyostationhotel.jp; 1-9-1 Marunouchi, Chiyoda-ku; r from ¥41,000; ❸✳@🛜; 🚉JR lines to Tokyo, Marunouchi south exit) occupies the south end of the building; to the north is **Tokyo Station Gallery** (www.ejrcf.or.jp/gallery; Tokyo Station, 1-9-1 Marunouchi, Chiyoda-ku; admission differs for each exhibition; ◷10am-6pm Tue-Thu, Sat & Sun, to 8pm Fri; ㉘JR lines to Tokyo, Marunouchi north exit), which hosts interesting exhibitions and the useful JR East Travel Service Center (p181). (東京国際フォーラム; ☎5221-9000; www.t-i-forum.co.jp; 3-5-1 Marunouchi, Chiyoda-ku; admission free; ㉘JR Yamanote line to Yūrakuchō, central exit)

Crafts Gallery   MUSEUM

5 ◉ Map p26, A1

Housed in a vintage red-brick building, this annex of MOMAT stages excellent changing exhibitions of *mingei* (folk crafts): ceramics, lacquerware, bamboo, textiles, dolls and much more. Artists range from living national treasures to contemporary artisans. The building was once the headquarters of the imperial guards, and was rebuilt after its destruction in WWII. (東京国立近代美術館 工芸館; www.momat.go.jp/english; 1 Kitanomaru-kōen, Chiyoda-ku; adult/child ¥210/70, 1st Sun of month free; ◷10am-5pm Tue-Sun; ⑤Tōzai line to Takebashi, exit 1b)

Nihombashi (Nihonbashi)   BRIDGE

6 ◉ Map p26, E2

Guarded by bronze lions and dragons, this handsome 1911-vintage granite bridge over Nihonbashi-gawa is sadly obscured by the overhead expressway. It's notable as the point from which all distances were measured during the Edo period and as the begin-

---

Understand
The Meiji Restoration

For 250 years the Tokugawa shoguns kept Japan almost entirely isolated. Then, in 1853, the black ships under the command of US Navy Commodore Matthew Perry sailed into Tokyo Bay demanding that Japan open itself to foreign trade. The humiliating acquiescence that followed fanned existing flames of antigovernment sentiment: a coalition of southern Japan *daimyō* (feudal lords) founded a movement (and army) to restore the emperor to power. In 1868, after months of civil war, the shogun stepped down and the 16-year-old Emperor Meiji was named head of state. Meiji moved the seat of imperial power from Kyoto to Edo, renaming the city Tokyo (Eastern Capital).

The Meiji Restoration had far-reaching social implications, as Japan opened up to the world and began to adopt technology as well as political and social ideas from the West. Marunouchi was established as the first business district in the modern sense, and a culture of white-collar workers in suit and tie commuting by streetcar grew up around it.

ning of the great trunk roads (the Tōkaidō, the Nikkō Kaidō etc) that took *daimyō* (feudal lords) between Edo and their home provinces. (日本橋; www.nihonbashi-tokyo.jp; S Ginza line to Mitsukoshimae, exits B5 & B6)

Eating

Hōnen Manpuku
JAPANESE $$

 7 Map p26, E2

Offering a riverside terrace in warmer months, Hōnen Manpuku's interior is dominated by giant *washi* (Japanese handmade paper) lanterns beneath which patrons tuck into bargain-priced beef or pork sukiyaki and other traditional dishes. Ingredients are sourced from gourmet retailers in Nihombashi. Lunchtime set menus are great value. (豊年萬福; ☑3277-3330; www.hounenmanpuku.jp; 1-8-16 Nihombashi-Muromachi, Chūō-ku; mains ¥1280-1850; ◷11.30am-2.30pm & 5-11pm Mon-Sat, 5-10pm Sun; S Ginza line to Mitsukoshimae, exit A1)

Tokyo Rāmen Street
RĀMEN $

8 Map p26, D3

Eight hand-picked *rāmen-ya* operate minibranches in this basement arcade on the Yaesu side of Tokyo Station. All the major styles are covered, from *shōyu* (soy-sauce base) to *tsukemen* (cold noodles served on the side). Long lines form outside the most popular but they tend to move quickly. (東京ラーメンストリート; www.tokyoeki-1bangai. co.jp/ramenstreet; B1 First Avenue Tokyo Station, 1-9-1 Marunouchi, Chiyoda-ku; rāmen from ¥800; ◷7.30am-10.30pm; ☒JR lines to Tokyo Station, Yaesu south exit)

Rose Bakery Marunouchi
BAKERY $

9 Map p26, C3

Tokyo has taken to Paris' Rose Bakery style of dining. Branches of this delicious organic cafe have popped up here in the Comme des Garçons boutique as well as at the same fashion company's Dover Street Market in Ginza and Isetan in Shinjuku. Vegetarians are well served but it is also for those who fancy a full English fry-up for weekend brunch. (ローズベーカリー 丸の内; ☑3212-1715; http://rosebakery.jp; Meiji-Yasada Bldg, 2-1-1 Marunouchi, Chiyoda-ku; cakes, quiches from ¥410, lunch sets ¥1350; ◷11am-7pm; S Chiyoda line to Nijūbashimae, exit 3;)

Meal MUJI Yūrakuchō
DELI $

Those who subscribe to the Muji lifestyle will be delighted to know that the 'no name brand' experience goes beyond neutral-toned notebooks, containers and linens. Located at its flagship store (see 14 Map p26, C4) Meal MUJI follows the 'simpler is better' mantra with fresh deli fare uncluttered by chemicals and unpronounceable ingredients. (MealMUJI有楽町; ☑5208-8241; www.muji.net/cafemeal/; 3-8-3 Marunouchi, Chiyoda-ku; meals from ¥780; ◷10am-9pm; ; ☒JR Yamanote line to Yūrakuchō, Kyōbashi exit)

Drinking

So Tired　BAR

10 📍 Map p26, C2

The best thing about this bar on the lively 7th floor of the Shin-Maru Building is that you can buy a drink at the counter and take it out to the terrace. The views aren't sky-high; instead you feel curiously suspended among the office towers, hovering over Tokyo Station below. (ソータイアード; ☏5220-1358; www.heads-west.com/shop/so-tired.html; 7th fl, Shin-Marunouchi Bldg, 1-5-1 Marunouchi, Chiyoda-ku; ⏰11am-4am Mon-Sat, to 11pm Sun; 🚉JR lines to Tokyo, Marunouchi north exit)

Manpuku Shokudō　IZAKAYA

11 📍 Map p26, C4

Down your beer or sake as trains rattle overhead on the tracks that span Harumi-dōri at Yūrakuchō. This convivial *izakaya* (Japanese pub-eatery), plastered with old movie posters, is open round the clock and has bags of atmosphere. (まんぷく食堂; ☏3211-6001; www.manpukushokudo.com; 2-4-1 Yūrakuchō, Chiyoda-ku; cover charge ¥300; ⏰24hr; 🚉JR Yamanote line to Yūrakuchō, central exit)

Shopping

Takashimaya　DEPARTMENT STORE

12 🔒 Map p26, E3

The design of Takashimaya's flagship store (1933) tips its pillbox hat to New York's Gilded Age with marble columns, chandeliers and uniformed female elevator operators announcing each floor in high-pitched singsong voices. Take your passport and you can get a free Shoppers Discount card giving you 5% off purchases over ¥3000. (高島屋; www.takashimaya.co.jp/tokyo/store_information; 2-4-1 Nihombashi, Chūō-ku; ⏰10am-8pm; 🚇Ginza line to Nihombashi, Takashimaya exit)

Coredo Muromachi　MALL

13 🔒 Map p26, E2

Spread over three buildings, this stylish new development hits its stride at Coredo Muromachi 3. It houses several well-curated floors of top-class Japanese-crafted goods, including cosmetics, fashion, homewares, eyeglasses and speciality food. (コレド室町; http://mi-mo.jp/pc/lng/eng/muromachi.

Local Life

Naka-dōri

Naka-dōri, which runs parallel to the palace between Hibiya and Ōtemachi Stations, is a pretty, tree-lined avenue with upscale boutiques and patio cafes. **Cafe Salvador** (Map p26, C3) www.cafecompany.co.jp/brands/salvador/marunouchi; 3-2-3 Marunouchi, Chiyoda-ku; ⏰7am-11pm Mon-Fri, 10am-11pm Sat, 10am-8pm Sun; 📶; 🚉JR Yūrakuchō line to Yūrakuchō, Kokusai Forum exit) is one place to try. It has cosy sofas and funky art on the walls.

Tokyo International Forum (p27)

html; 2-2-1 Nihonbashi-Muromachi, Chūō-ku; ⏱ most shops 11am-7pm; Ⓢ Ginza line to Mitsukoshimae, exit A4)

Muji

CLOTHING, HOMEWARES

14 🔒 Map p26, C4

The flagship store of the famously understated brand sells elegant, simple clothing, accessories and homewares. There are scores of other outlets across Tokyo, including a good one in Tokyo Midtown, but the Yūrakuchō store also has bicycle rental and a great cafeteria. (無印良品; www.muji.com; 3-8-3 Marunouchi, Chiyoda-ku; ⏱ 10am-9pm; Ⓡ JR Yamanote line to Yūrakuchō, Kyōbashi exit)

Tokyo Character Street

TOYS

15 🔒 Map p26, D3

From Doraemon to Domo-kun, Hello Kitty to Ultraman, Japan knows *kawaii* (cute) and how to merchandise it. In the basement on the Yaesu side of Tokyo Station, some 15 Japanese TV networks and toy manufacturers operate stalls selling official plush toys, sweets, accessories and the all-important miniature character to dangle from your mobile phone. (東京キャラクターストリート; www.tokyoeki-1bangai.co.jp; B1 First Avenue Tokyo Station, 1-9-1 Marunouchi, Chiyoda-ku; ⏱ 10am-8.30pm; Ⓡ JR lines to Tokyo Station, Yaesu exit)

Explore

Tsukiji Market & Ginza

Ginza is Tokyo's most polished neighbourhood, a fashion centre for more than a century, resplendent with department stores, galleries, gardens and teahouses. The city's kabuki (traditional Japanese performing art) theatre, Kabuki-za, is here, as are many of Tokyo's most celebrated restaurants. A short walk away is a luxury commercial centre of a different sort: Tsukiji Market.

The Sights in a Day

Get an early start – 4am if you want to catch the tuna auction – at **Tsukiji Market** (p34). After the auction, go for sushi breakfast at **Daiwa Sushi** (p40) and explore the outer market until the Seafood Intermediate Wholesalers Area opens to the public at 9am. If you'd prefer not to get up before dawn, aim to get to the Seafood Intermediate Wholesalers Area when it opens at 9am and then hit the outer market and grab sushi for lunch.

After lunch, walk down to the landscaped garden **Hama-rikyū Onshi-teien** (p39) and have tea in the garden's teahouse. Then gallery-hop and window-shop your way through Ginza. Don't miss **Mitsukoshi** (p43) and its famous basement food hall. In the late afternoon, see a kabuki performance at Tokyo's most famous theatre, **Kabuki-za** (p36).

If you do the full show at Kabuki-za, your dinner will be a *bentō* (boxed meal), traditionally eaten during intermission. Otherwise, check out trendy 'standing-restaurant' **Ore-no-dashi** (p40) or go for a proper sit-down meal at reasonably priced *kaiseki* (haute cuisine) restaurant **Maru** (p41).

Top Sights

Tsukiji Market (p34)

Kabuki-za (p36)

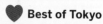 **Best of Tokyo**

Architecture
Nakagin Capsule Tower (p40)

Parks & Gardens
Hama-rikyū Onshi-teien (p39)

Galleries & Museums
Shiseido Gallery (p39)

Food
Kyūbey (p40)

Daiwa Sushi (p40)

Shopping
Dover Street Market (p42)

Takumi (p42)

Getting There

Train The JR Yamanote line stops at Shimbashi Station.

S **Subway** Ginza, Hibiya and Marunouchi lines stop at Ginza Station; Hibiya line continues to Higashi-Ginza and Tsukiji, take the Ginza line to Shimbashi and Ōedo line to Shiodome and Tsukijishijō.

Ferry Tokyo Cruise water buses dock at Hama-rikyū Onshi-teien.

Top Sights
Tsukiji Market

This is the world's biggest seafood market, moving an astounding 1800 tonnes of seafood a day. You'll find all manner of fascinating creatures passing through, but it is the *maguro* (bluefin tuna) that has emerged the star. Even if you don't arrive at dawn for the tuna auction, you can still get a flavour of the frenetic atmosphere of the market. The whole show will pack up and move to a new location in Toyosu, on Tokyo Bay, in November 2016 (see p40). The bustling outer market will remain. Admission is free.

東京都中央卸売市場

Map p38, C4

☏ 3261-8326

www.tsukiji-market.or.jp

5-2-1 Tsukiji, Chūō-ku

🕐 5am-1pm, closed Sun, most Wed & public holidays

Ⓢ Hibiya line to Tsukiji, exit 1

Tsukiji Market

Don't Miss

Tuna Auction

Bidding for prized *maguro* – which can sell for more than US$10,000 each – starts at 5am. Up to 120 visitors a day in two shifts are allowed to watch the auction from a gallery between 5.25am and 6.15am. It's first come, first served; register by 5am at the **Fish Information Center** (おさかな普及センター, Osakana Fukyū Senta; Map p38; Kachidoki Gate, 6-20-5 Tsukiji, Chūō-ku), at the northwest corner of the market.

Seafood Intermediate Wholesalers Area

Here you can see a truly global haul of sea creatures, from gloriously magenta octopuses to gnarled turban shells. All are laid out for buyers in styrofoam crates – it's a photographer's paradise. This part of the market opens to the public from 9am, and you'll want to get here as close to then as possible; by 11am most stalls are cleaning up.

Outer Market

The outer market, open roughly 5am to 2pm on market days, is where rows of vendors hawk related goods such as dried fish and seaweed, rubber boots and crockery. It's far more pedestrian friendly. It is also where you'll find the market's Shintō shrine, **Namiyoke-jinja**, the deity of which protects seafarers.

Forklifts & Handcarts

Tsukiji is a working market, and you need to exercise caution to avoid getting in the way. Forklifts and handcarts perform a perfect high-speed choreography not accounting for the odd tourist. Don't come in large groups, with small children or in nice shoes, and definitely don't touch anything you don't plan to buy.

☑ Top Tips

▶ As well as regular market holidays, the tuna auction may close to visitors during busy periods (such as December and January); see the website for details.

▶ The line to register for the tuna auction starts forming before 5am; to make sure you get in, get there by 4am. Public transport doesn't start early enough, so you'll have to take a taxi or hang out nearby all night.

▶ Get a map at the **Tourist Information Center** (Map p38; ☎6264-1925; www.tsukiji.or.jp; 4-16-2 Tsukiji, Chuo-ku; ◷9.30am-1.30pm Mon-Sat, 10am-2pm Sun; Ⓢ Hibiya line to Tsukiji, exit 1) inside the outer market.

✕ Take a Break

Get a caffeine kick at **Turret Coffee** (2-12-6 Tsukiji, Chūō-ku; ◷7am-6pm Mon-Sat, noon-6pm Sun; Ⓢ Hibiya line to Tsukiji, exit 2).

Go for sushi breakfast at Daiwa Sushi (p40).

Top Sights
Kabuki-za

Dramatic, intensely visual kabuki is Japan's most recognised art form. It developed during the reign of the shogun and was shaped by the decadent tastes of the increasingly wealthy merchant class of Edo (old Tokyo under the shogun) – resulting in the breathtaking costumes and elaborate stagecraft that characterise the form. Kabuki-za is Tokyo's kabuki theatre. Established in 1889, the theatre reopened after a lengthy reconstruction in 2013. The new building, designed by architect Kuma Kengo, has a flamboyant facade and scarlet and gold throughout.

歌舞伎座

Map p38, C2

☎ 3545-6800

www.kabuki-bito.jp/eng

4-12-15 Ginza, Chūō-ku

tickets ¥4000-20,000, single-act tickets ¥800-2000

🚇 Hibiya line to Higashi-Ginza, exit 3

Kabuki-za

Don't Miss

The Actors

Kabuki actors train from childhood and descendants of the great Edo-era actors still grace the stage, as sons follow their fathers into the *yago* (kabuki acting house). These stars enjoy a celebrity on par with screen actors; some have earned the status of 'living treasure'. Only men appear in kabuki, and actors who specialise in portraying women are called *onnagata*.

The Fans

At pivotal moments enthusiastic fans shout out the name of the *yago* of the actor – an act called *kakegoe*.

The Plays

During several centuries, kabuki has developed a repertoire of popular themes, such as famous historical accounts, the conflict between love and loyalty and stories of love-suicide. A full kabuki performance comprises several acts, usually from different plays, so you should get a sampling of various themes and styles.

The Visual Impact

There is no pretence of reality in kabuki; it's ruled by aesthetics and plays to the senses rather than the intellect. Kabuki has been likened to a moving wood-block print, and when the actors pause in dramatic poses – called *mie* – the whole stage really does look fit to be framed.

The Stage Design

The kabuki stage employs a number of unique devices, such as the *hanamichi* (the walkway that extends into the audience), which is used for dramatic entrances and exits. Naturally the best seats are those that line the *hanamichi*.

☑ Top Tips

▶ If you purchased a ticket online, look for the ticket dispensers in front of the theatre and in the basement passage from the subway station. Just insert the credit card you used to purchase the ticket.

▶ Rent a headset for explanations in English; the recording begins 10 minutes before each act, with background information about the play.

▶ Single-act 'makumi' tickets (p165) can be purchased from the box office.

✕ Take a Break

During intermission (usually 30 minutes), it's tradition to eat a *bentō* at the theatre. Purchase one (around ¥1000) from any of the concession stands inside the theatre or in the basement passage in the subway station. You could also pack a meal with goodies culled from the *depachika* (basement food hall) at Mitsukoshi (p43).

400 m
0.2 miles

HATCHŌBORI

S Hatchōbori

Shin-Ōhashi-dōri

SHINTOMI

Shintomi-chō

CHŪŌ-KU

Ginza Marronnier-dōri

Shōwa-dōri

S Ginza-itchōme

TSUKIJI

S Tsukiji

Harumi-dōri

Tsukiji
Outer
Market

Fish ℹ
Information
Center

Kachidoki-mon

Tokyo Cruise Route

Sumida-gawa (Sumida River)

KACHIDOKI

S Kachidoki-bashi

New Toyosu
Market (2km)

GINZA

S Hibiya Yūrakuchō

Harumi-dōri

S Ginza

Namiki-dōri

Chūō-dōri

15

13

11

Miyuki-dōri

Sony-dōri

Sukiyabashi-dōri

Hanatsubaki-dōri

14

7

16 $

18

5

3

Ginza
Graphic
Gallery

Ginza
Graphic
Gallery

Shiseido
Gallery

2

12

8

17 Ginza

Matsuya-dōri

Mihara-dōri

Kabuki-za

Higashi-
Ginza

S Higashi-
Ginza

Information
Centre Plat
Tsukijishijō Tsukiji

ℹ

Shuto Expwy No1

Tsukiji-dōri

Nakagin 4
Capsule
Tower

S Shimbashi

S Shimbashi

S Shiodome

Shimbashi

SHIMBASHI

UCHISAIWAI-CHŌ

S Uchisaiwaichō

10

Sotobori-dōri

Hibiya-dōri

9 ✕

✕ 6

Tsukiji Market
S Tsukiji Market

Tokyo
Cruise
Pier

Hama-rikyū
Onshi-teien

1

Kaigan-dōri

Haneda
Airport (12km)

Sights

Hama-rikyū Onshi-teien

GARDENS

1 ⊙ Map p38, B4

This beautiful garden, one of Tokyo's finest, is all that remains of a shogunal palace that once extended into the area now occupied by Tsukiji Market. The main features are a large duck pond with an island that's home to a charming tea pavilion, **Nakajima no Ochaya** (中島の御茶屋; www.tokyo-park.or.jp/park/format/restaurant028.html; 1-1 Hama-rikyū Onshi-teien, Chūō-ku; tea set ¥500; ⊙9am-4.30pm; ◨Ōedo line to Shiodome, exit A1), as well as some wonderfully manicured trees (black pine, Japanese apricot, hydrangeas etc), some of which are hundreds of years old. (浜離宮恩賜庭園; Detached Palace Garden; www.tokyo-park.or.jp/park/format/index028.html; 1-1 Hama-rikyū-teien, Chūō-ku; adult/child ¥300/free; ⊙9am-5pm; ⓢŌedo line to Shiodome, exit A1)

Shiseido Gallery

GALLERY

2 ⊙ Map p38, B2

The cosmetics company Shiseido runs its experimental art space out of the basement of its Shiseido Parlour complex of cafes and restaurants. An ever-changing selection, particularly of installation pieces, lends itself well to the gallery's high ceiling. (資生堂ギャラリー; ☏3572-3901; www.shiseido.co.jp/e/gallery/html; Basement fl, 8-8-3 Ginza, Chūō-ku; admission free; ⊙11am-7pm Tue-Sat, to 6pm Sun; ⓢGinza line to Shimbashi, exit 1 or 3)

Ginza Graphic Gallery

GALLERY

3 ⊙ Map p38, B2

This gallery has monthly changing exhibits of graphic arts from mostly Japanese artists, but with the occasional Western artist. It focuses on advertising and poster art. The annual Tokyo Art Directors Conference exhibition takes place here in July. (ギンザ・グラフィック・ギャラリー; ☏3571-5206;

Understand

Trendsetting Ginza

In the 1870s, Gi&nza was the first neighbourhood in Tokyo to modernise, welcoming Western-style brick buildings, the city's first department stores, gas lamps and other harbingers of globalisation – and it's been a fashion centre ever since. In the 1920s, *moga* (modern girls) cut their hair short, wore trousers and walked arm in arm with *mobo* (modern boys) through the Ginza.

Today, other shopping districts rival Ginza in opulence, vitality and popularity, but it retains a distinct snob value: all the major international fashion houses have lavish boutiques here. Ginza also remains the launching pad for foreign brands making their debut in Japan: McDonald's (1971), Starbucks (1996) and H&M (2008) all opened their first shops in the neighbourhood.

Understand
Tsukiji Market Moving

Tsukiji Market, which replaced the original Nihombashi Market in 1935, is indeed moving to Toyosu in November 2016. The controversial move has been in the works for years, delayed due to the need to clean up the new site – where a gas plant once stood – on an artificially constructed island in Tokyo Bay. New Toyosu Market, as the market will be called, will have state-of-the-art facilities, including temperature-controlled rooms, as well as a viewing area for tourists.

www.dnp.co.jp/gallery/ggg; 7-7-2 Ginza, Chūō-ku; admission free; ⊙11am-7pm Tue-Fri, to 6pm Sat; §Ginza line to Ginza, exit A2)

Nakagin Capsule Tower
ARCHITECTURE

4 Map p38, B3

A Facebook campaign has been started by some residents and fans to save Kurokawa Kisho's early-1970s building, which is a seminal work of Metabolist architecture. The tower's self-contained pods, which can be removed whole from a central core and replaced else-where, are in various states of decay but it's still a very impressive design. It's possible to arrange to stay here via Airbnb. (中銀カプセルタワー; www.nakagincapsule.com; 8-16-10 Ginza, Chūō-ku; §Ōedo line to Tsukijishijō, exit A3)

Eating

Kyūbey
SUSHI $$$

5 Map p38, B2

Since 1936, Kyūbey's quality and presentation has won it a moneyed and celebrity clientele. Even so, this is a supremely foreigner-friendly and relaxed restaurant. Expect personal greetings in English by the owner Imada-san, and his team of talented chefs, who will make and serve your sushi, piece by piece. (久兵衛; ☏3571-6523; www.kyubey.jp; 8-7-6 Ginza, Chūō-ku; sushi sets lunch ¥5000-8400, dinner from ¥10,500; ⊙11.30am-2pm & 5-10pm Mon-Sat; §Ginza line to Shimbashi, exit 3)

Daiwa Sushi
SUSHI $$

6 Map p38, C4

Waits of over one hour are common-place at Tsukiji's most famous sushi bar, after which you'll be expected to eat and run. But it's all worth it once your first piece of delectable sushi hits the counter. Unless you're comfortable ordering in Japanese, the standard set (seven *nigiri*, plus *maki* and miso soup) is a good bet; there's a picture menu. (大和寿司; ☏3547-6807; Bldg 6, 5-2-1 Tsukiji, Chūō-ku; sushi sets ¥3500; ⊙5am-1.30pm Mon-Sat, closed occasional Wed; §Ōedo line to Tsukijishijomae, exit A1)

Ore-no-dashi
JAPANESE $

7 Map p38, B2

The Ore-no chain – where you stand to eat gourmet dishes prepared by skilled chefs at bargain prices – has been a massive success in Ginza. This one specialises in *oden* – delicious morsels simmered in *dashi* (fish) stock. There are seats here too and a good wine list. (俺のだし; 03-3571-6762; www.oreno. co.jp/en/eaterycat/dashi; 7-6-6 Ginza; dishes from ¥380-1480; ☺5pm-2am Mon-Fri, 4-11pm Sat & Sun; ⑤Ginza line to Ginza, exit A2)

Maru
JAPANESE $$$

 8   Map p38, C2

Maru offers a contemporary take on *kaiseki* fine dining. The chefs are young and inventive, and the appealing space is dominated by a long, wooden, open kitchen counter across which you can watch them work. Its good-value lunches offer a choice of mainly fish dishes. (銀座圓; ☎5537-7420; www.maru-mayfont.jp/ginza; 2nd fl, Ichigo Ginza 612 Bldg, 6-12-15 Ginza, Chūō-ku; lunch/dinner from ¥1100/6000; ☺11.30am-2pm & 5.30-9pm Mon-Sat; ⑤Ginza line to Ginza, exit A3)

Trattoria Tsukiji Paradiso!
ITALIAN $$

 9   Map p38, D4

Paradise for food lovers, indeed. This charming, aqua-painted trattoria plays on its proximity to Tsukiji with seafood pasta dishes that will make you want to lick the plate clean. Its signature linguine is packed with shellfish in a scrumptious tomato, chilli and garlic sauce. Lunch (from ¥980) is a bargain; book for dinner. (☎3545-5550; www. tsukiji-paradiso.com; 6-27-3 Tsukiji, Chūō-ku;

mains ¥1500-3600; ☺11am-2pm & 6-10pm; ⑤Hibiya line to Tsukiji, exit 2)

Drinking

Kagaya
IZAKAYA

10 Map p38, A3

It is safe to say that there is no other bar owner in Tokyo who can match Mark Kagaya for brilliant lunacy. His side-splitting antics are this humble *izakaya*'s star attraction, although his mum's nourishing home cooking also hits the spot. Bookings are essential. (加賀屋; ☎3591-2347; www1.ocn. ne.jp/~kagayayy/index.html; B1 fl, Hanasada Bldg, 2-15-12 Shimbashi, Minato-ku; ☺7pm-midnight Mon-Sat; ℝJR Yamanote line to Shimbashi, Shimbashi exit)

Cha Ginza
TEAHOUSE

11   Map p38, B2

At this slick, contemporary tearoom, it costs ¥600 for either a cup of

Local Life
Namiki-dōri

Namiki-dōri (Map p38, C1) is Tokyo's most exclusive nightlife strip, where velvet drapes blot out the windows and elegant women dressed in kimonos wait on company execs and politicians in members-only bars and clubs. Stroll through in the evening and you might catch a glimpse of this secretive world.

perfectly prepared *matcha* (green tea), and a small cake or two, or for a choice of *sencha* (premium green tea). Buy your token for tea at the shop on the ground floor which sells top-quality teas from various growing regions in Japan. (茶・銀座; www. uogashi-meicha.co.jp/shop/ginza; 5-5-6 Ginza, Chūō-ku; tea set ¥500; ⏰11am-6pm, shop until 7pm Tue-Sun; Ⓢ Ginza line to Ginza, exit B3)

Cafe de l'Ambre
CAFE

12 Map p38, B3

The sign over the door here reads 'Coffee Only' but, oh, what a selection. In business since 1948, l'Ambre specialises in aged beans from all over the world, which the owner still roasts himself. (カフェ・ド・ランブル; ☎3571-1551; www.h6.dion.ne.jp/~lambre; 8-10-15 Ginza, Chūō-ku; coffee from ¥650; ⏰noon-10pm Mon-Sat, to 7pm Sun; Ⓡ Ginza line to Ginza, exit A4)

Shopping

Sony Building
ELECTRONICS

13 🔒 Map p38, B1

Where Sony shows off and sells its latest digital and electronic gizmos. Kids will love the free Playstation games, while adults tend to lose an hour or so perusing all the latest audio and video accessories. (ソニービル; ☎3573-2371; www.sonybuilding.jp; 5-3-1 Ginza, Chūō-ku; ⏰11am-7pm; 📶; Ⓢ Ginza, Hibiya or Marunouchi line to Ginza, exit B9)

Takumi
CRAFTS

14 🔒 Map p38, B2

You'll be hard-pressed to find a more elegant selection of traditional folk crafts, including toys, textiles and ceramics, from around Japan. Ever thoughtful, the shop also encloses information detailing the origin and background of the pieces if you make a purchase. (たくみ; ☎3571-2017; www. ginza-takumi.co.jp; 8-4-2 Ginza, Chūō-ku; ⏰11am-7pm Mon-Sat; Ⓢ Ginza line to Shimbashi, exit 5)

Akomeya
FOOD

15 🔒 Map p38, C1

Rice is at the core of Japanese cuisine and drink. This stylish store sells not only many types of the grain but also products made from it (such as sake), a vast range of quality cooking ingredients and a choice collection of kitchen, home and bath items. (☎6758-0271; www.akomeya.jp; 2-2-6 Ginza, Chūō-ku; ⏰ shop 11am-9pm, restaurant 11.30am-10pm; Ⓢ Yūrakuchō line to Ginza-itchome, exit 4)

Dover Street Market Ginza
FASHION

16 🔒 Map p38, B2

A department store as envisioned by Kawakubo Rei (of Comme des Garçons), DSM has seven floors of avant-garde brands, including several Japanese labels and everything in the Comme des Garcons line-up. The quirky art installations alone make it worth the visit. (DSM; ☎6228-5080;

Hama-rikyū Onshi-teien (p39)

http://ginza.doverstreetmarket.com; 6-9-5 Ginza, Chūō-ku; ⊙11am-8pm Sun-Thu, to 9pm Fri & Sat; **S** Ginza line to Ginza, exit A2)

Mitsukoshi

DEPARTMENT STORE

17 🅐 Map p38, C2

One of Ginza's grande dames, Mitsukoshi embodies the essence of the Tokyo department store, and it gleams after a recent renovation. Don't miss the basement food hall. (三越; www.mitsukoshi. co.jp; 4-6-16 Ginza, Chūō-ku; ⊙10am-8pm; **S** Ginza line to Ginza, exits A7 & A11)

Uniqlo

FASHION

18 🅐 Map p38, B2

This now-global brand has made its name by sticking to the basics and tweaking them with style. Offering inexpensive, quality clothing, this is the Tokyo flagship store with 11 floors and items you won't find elsewhere. (ユニクロ; www.uniqlo.com; 5-7-7 Ginza, Chūō-ku; ⊙11am-9pm; **S** Ginza line to Ginza, exit A2)

Top Sights
Sumo at Ryōgoku Kokugikan

Getting There

🚃 **Train** Take the JR Sōbu line to Ryōgoku and use the west exit; the stadium is a two-minute walk away.

Ⓢ **Subway** The Ōedo line also stops at Ryōgoku.

Travellers visiting Tokyo in January, May or September should not miss the opportunity to attend one of the 15-day sumo tournaments at the national stadium, Ryōgoku Kokugikan. Never mind if you're a sports fan or not, ancient sumo is just as captivating for its spectacle and ritual. Ringside tickets cost ¥14,800, but reserved arena seats start from ¥3800. Same-day unreserved seats can be bought from the stadium box office for only ¥2200. During the rest of the year, catch the big boys in action at one of the neighbourhood stables.

Sumo wrestlers at Ryōgoku Kokugikan

Don't Miss

The Ritual

Sumo was originally part of a ritual prayer to the gods for a good harvest. While it has obviously evolved, it remains deeply connected to Japan's Shintō tradition. You'll see a roof suspended over the *dōyo* (ring) that resembles that of a shrine. Before bouts, *rikishi* (wrestlers) rinse their mouths with water and toss salt into the ring – both are purification rituals.

Makuuchi Entering the Ring

Things really pick up at 3.45pm when the *makuuchi* (top-tier) wrestlers perform their ceremonial entrance, wearing colourful, embroidered aprons. This is followed by the grand entrance of the *yokozuna* (the top of the top) complete with sword-bearing attendants.

The Yokozuna

In order to achieve this highest rank a wrestler must win two consecutive tournaments and be considered, in the eyes of the Sumo Association, to embody certain traditional values. The *yokozuna* wrestle in the final, most exciting, bouts of the day. You'll also see portraits of past champions hanging around the stadium and at the Sumo Museum attached to the stadium.

Nearby: Arashio-beya

If you're not visiting during a tournament, you can watch an early-morning practice at **Arashio Stable** (荒汐部屋, Arashio-beya; ☎3666-7646; www.arashio.net/tour_e.html; 2-47-2 Hama-chō, Nihombashi, Chūō-ku; admission free; ⑤Toei Shinjuku line to Hamachō, exit A2), one of many stables where wrestlers sleep, eat and train. See the website for information about visiting and etiquette.

両国国技館, Ryōgoku Sumo Stadium

☎3623-5111

www.sumo.or.jp

1-3-28 Yokoami, Sumida-ku

admission ¥2200-14,800

☑ Top Tips

▶ On the last days of the tournament, get in line by 6am to score a same-day ticket.

▶ Rent a radio (¥100, plus ¥2000 deposit) to hear the action in English.

✗ Take a Break

Chanko-nabe, a protein-rich stew, is what the wrestlers eat. Sample it at **Chanko Kaijō** (ちゃんこ会場; chanko-nabe ¥250; ☉noon-4pm) in the stadium's basement, or at **Tomoegata** (巴潟; www.tomoegata.com; 2-17-6 Ryōgoku, Sumida-ku; lunch/dinner from ¥860/3130; ☉11.30am-2pm & 5-11pm; ☒JR Sōbu line to Ryōgoku, east exit), near JR Ryōgoku Station.

Explore

Roppongi & Akasaka

Roppongi is Tokyo's most exciting neighbourhood. Once notorious for low-brow nightlife, Roppongi is now wallowing in sophistication, with the shops, restaurants and museums to prove it. Must-sees include the future-forward microcity, Roppongi Hills, and its contemporary-art museum, Mori Art Museum. But Roppongi hasn't given up its night-life crown – it remains one of the best places to party in Asia.

FRANK DEIM/GETTY IMAGES ©

The Sights in a Day

Start the day in Shiba-kōen, taking the subway to Ake-banebashi. Situated on the edge of this leafy park is **Zōjō-ji** (p53), one of Tokyo's most important temples. This is also where you'll spot **Tokyo Tower** (p52), which offers views over the city. Then settle in for a long, leisurely lunch of Japanese haute cuisine at **Tofuya-Ukai** (p54).

Take a cab to **Tokyo Midtown** (p52) in Roppongi. Wander through the halls and garden, taking in an exhibition at **21_21 Design Sight** (p52) or the **Suntory Museum of Art** (p52). Then walk over to **Roppongi Hills** (p48) – the neighbourhood's other city within a city. Budget at least an hour or two for the **Mori Art Museum** (p49).

Have dinner at one of Rop-pongi's lively *izakaya* (Japanese-style pubs), such as **Jōmon** (p55) or **Gonpachi** (p56). Then pick your pleasure from the neighbourhood's overwhelming nightlife options: will you bar-hop? Dance till dawn? Catch a show or sing your heart out at karaoke? Don't worry, it's possible to pick more than one.

👁 Top Sights
Roppongi Hills (p48)

💜 Best of Tokyo

Temples & Shrines
Zōjō-ji (p53)

Galleries & Museums
Mori Art Museum (p49)

21_21 Design Sight (p52)

Food
Kikunoi (p54)

Tofuya-Ukai (p54)

Jōmon (p55)

Shopping
Souvenir from Tokyo (p59)

Nightlife & Live Music
SuperDeluxe (p56)

Pink Cow (p56)

Festa Iikura (p56)

Getting There

S Subway The Hibiya and Ōedo lines both stop at Roppongi. The Hibiya line is most convenient for Roppongi Hills; the Ōedo line for Tokyo Midtown. The Hibiya line continues to Kamiyachō; the Ōedo line goes to Akebanebashi. The Chiyoda line services Nogi-zaka and Akasaka.

Top Sights
Roppongi Hills

Roppongi Hills, completed in 2003, sprawls more than 11 hectares and is home to the city's leading contemporary-art museum, Mori Art Museum, a sky-high observatory, shops galore, dozens of restaurants and even a formal garden. It's imposing, upmarket and polarising – an architectural marvel, a grand vision realised or a crass shrine to conspicuous consumption? Explore the towers and corridors of this urban maze and decide for yourself, but you can't understand contemporary Tokyo without stopping here.

六本木ヒルズ

◉ Map p50, C5

www.roppongihills.com/en

6-chōme Roppongi, Minato-ku

🕙 11am-11pm

Ⓢ Hibiya line to Roppongi, exit 1

Mohri Garden

Don't Miss

Mori Art Museum

The **Mori Art Museum** (森美術館; www.mori.art. museum; 52nd & 53rd fls, Mori Tower, Roppongi Hills; adult/student/child ¥1500/1000/500; ⏰10am-10pm Wed-Mon, to 5pm Tue, Sky Deck 10am-10pm; ⓢHibiya line to Roppongi, exit 1) has no permanent exhibition; instead, large-scale, original shows introduce major local and global artists and movements. Recent exhibitions have focused on the works of Chinese artist and dissident Ai Weiwei and native son Murakami Takashi.

Tokyo City View

Admission to the Mori Art Museum is shared with **Tokyo City View** (東京シティビュー; ☎6406-6652; www.roppongihills.com/tcv/en; 52nd fl, Mori Tower, Roppongi Hills, 6-10-1 Roppongi, Minato-ku; incl with admission to Mori Art Museum, observatory only adult/student/child ¥1500/1000/500; ⏰10am-11pm Mon-Thu & Sun, to 1am Fri & Sat; ⓢHibiya line to Roppongi, exit 1), the observatory that wraps itself around the 52nd floor, 250m high. The view is particularly spectacular at night. Weather permitting, you can also pop out to the rooftop **Sky Deck**.

Public Art

The open-air plaza near the street entrance is the lucky home of one of Louise Bourgeois' giant *Maman* spider sculptures. It has an amusing way of messing with the scale of the buildings, especially in photos. There are other sculptural wonders scattered around the complex, too.

Mohri Garden

This landscaped garden is modelled after those popular during the Edo period (1603-1868). When juxtaposed with the gleaming towers, it creates a fascinating study of luxury then and now. Look for the cherry trees in spring.

☑ Top Tips

▶ Save your ticket stub from the Mori Art Museum to get discounted admission at the Suntory Museum of Art or the National Art Center Tokyo.

▶ Unlike most museums, Mori Art Museum is open late – until 10pm every day except Tuesdays.

▶ Keep an eye out for events, especially in the summer, at Roppongi Hills Arena, an open-air space nestled in the middle of the complex.

▶ In winter months look for beautiful illuminations along Keyaki-zaka, on the southern edge of the complex.

✕ Take a Break

Start the day with brunch at Lauderdale (p55) on Keyaki-zaka.

Hip night spot Super-Deluxe (p56) is just down the street.

TBS Broadcasting Center

🔒 27

10 ✖

Galen-higashi-dōri

Loop Rd No 3

Nogi-jinja 8 ◎

Nogizaka Ⓢ

21_21 Design Sight 1 ◉

Hinokichō-kōen

Aoyama-reien (Aoyama Cemetery)

Midtown Garden

2 ◎

Suntory Museum of Art

◎ 3 Tokyo Midtown

National Art Center Tokyo

6 ◎

Seijōki-dōri

Ⓢ Roppongi

Aoyama-bochi-dōri (Cherry St)

Aoyama-kōen

23 ☕

Roppongi Crossing

Roppongi-dōri

15 ☕

20 ☕

Ⓢ Roppongi

ROPPONGI

14 ✖ ✪ 26

25 ✪

18 ☕

Shuto Expwy No 3

16 ✖

Ⓢ 17

Mohri Garden

✖ 12

Imoarai-zaka

Galen-nishi-dōri

21 ✖

TV Asahi

✖ 13 ◉ **Roppongi Hills**

Keyaki-zaka

Azabu-Jūban-dōri

Roppongi Hills

Torii-zaka

NISHI-AZABU

TV Asahi-dōri

ROPPONGI 6-CHŌME

E | **F** | **G** | **H**

Ⓢ Akasaka

Tokyo
Broadcasting
Station

Ⓢ Tameike-
sannō

24 ✪

N 0 ————————— 400 m
0 ————————— 0.2 miles

KASUMIGASEKI

Sotobori-dōri   Toranomon Ⓢ

AKASAKA

Tamachi-dōri

Shuto Expwy No 3

US
Embassy

Toranomon
Hospital

TORANOMON

Sakurada-dōri

Ark
Hills

Hotel
Ōkura

◎7
Musée
Tomo

29 🔒

Toranomon 9
Hills ◎

🍴
22

Ⓢ Roppongi-
itchōme

Ⓢ Kamiyachō

Shuto Expwy No 2

AZABUDAI

✉
🍴19

Sakurada-dōri

Tokyo
Tower
◎
4

11
✕

MINATO-KU

5
Zōjō-ji ◎ Shiba-
kōen

28
🔒▸

**HIGASHI-
AZABU**

Sights

21_21 Design Sight
MUSEUM

1 ◎ Map p50, C2

An exhibition and discussion space dedicated to all forms of design, the 21_21 Design Sight acts as a beacon for local art enthusiasts, whether they be designers themselves or simply onlookers. The striking concrete and glass building, bursting out of the ground at sharp angles, was designed by Pritzker Prize–winning architect Andō Tadao. (21_21デザインサイト; ☎3475-2121; www.2121designsight.jp; Tokyo Midtown, 9-7-6 Akasaka, Minato-ku; adult/child ¥1000/free; ⏰11am-8pm Wed-Mon; ⓢŌedo line to Roppongi, exit 8)

Suntory Museum of Art
MUSEUM

2 ◎ Map p50, C2

Since its original 1961 opening, the Suntory Museum of Art has subscribed to an underlying philosophy of lifestyle art. Rotating exhibitions focus on the beauty of useful things: Japanese ceramics, lacquerware, glass, dyeing, weaving and such. Its current Midtown digs, designed by architect Kuma Kengō, are both understated and breathtaking. (サントリー美術館; ☎3479-8600; www.suntory.com/sma; 4th fl, Tokyo Midtown, 9-7-4 Akasaka, Minato-ku; admission varies, children & junior-high-school students free; ⏰10am-6pm Sun-Thu, to 8pm Fri & Sat; ⓡŌedo line to Roppongi, exit 8)

Tokyo Midtown
LANDMARK

3 ◎ Map p50, C3

With a similar design and urban-planning blueprint to the one that made Roppongi Hills so successful, this sleek complex brims with sophisticated bars, restaurants, shops, art galleries, a hotel and leafy public spaces. Escalators ascend alongside human-made waterfalls of rock and glass, bridges in the air are lined with backlit *washi* (Japanese handmade paper) and planters full of soaring bamboo draw your eyes through skylights to the lofty heights of the towers above. (東京ミッドタウン; www.tokyo-midtown.com/en; 9-7 Akasaka, Minato-ku; ⏰11am-11pm; ⓢŌedo line to Roppongi, exit 8)

Tokyo Tower
TOWER

4 ◎ Map p50, G5

Something of a shameless tourist trap, this 1958-vintage tower remains a beloved symbol of the city's post-WWII rebirth. At 333m it's 13m taller than the Eiffel Tower, which was the inspiration for its design. It's also painted bright orange and white in order to comply with international aviation safety regulations.

The main observation deck is at 145m (there's another 'special' deck at 250m). There are loftier views at the more expensive Tokyo Sky Tree. (東京タワー; www.tokyotower.co.jp/english; 4-2-8 Shiba-kōen, Minato-ku; adult/child main deck ¥900/400, plus special deck ¥1600/800; ⏰observation deck 9am-10pm; ⓡŌedo line to Akabanebashi, Akabanebashi exit)

Wooden votive tablet at Zōjō-ji

Zōjō-ji

BUDDHIST TEMPLE

5 ◉ Map p50, H5

One of the most important temples of the Jōdō (Pure Land) sect of Buddhism, Zōjō-ji dates from 1393 and was the funerary temple of the Tokugawa regime. It's an impressive sight, particularly the main gate, **Sangedatsumon** (解脱門), constructed in 1605, with its three sections designed to symbolise the three stages one must pass through to achieve nirvana. The **Daibonsho** (Big Bell; 1673) is a 15-tonne whopper considered one of the great three bells of the Edo period. (増上寺; ☏ 3432-1431; www.zojoji.or.jp/en/index.html; 4-7-35 Shiba-kōen, Minato-ku; admission free; ☺ dawn-dusk; S Ōedo line to Daimon, exit A3)

National Art Center Tokyo

MUSEUM

6 ◉ Map p50, B3

Designed by Kurokawa Kishō, this architectural beauty has no permanent collection, but boasts the country's largest exhibition space for visiting shows, which have included Renoir, Modigliani and the Japan Media Arts Festival. You can also admire the building's awesome undulating glass facade, its cafes atop giant inverted cones and the great gift shop Souvenir From Tokyo (p59). (国立新美術館; ☏ 5777-8600; www.nact.jp; 7-22-1 Roppongi, Minato-ku; admission varies by exhibition; ☺ 10am-6pm Wed, Thu & Sat-Mon, to 8pm Fri; S Chiyoda line to Nogizaka, exit 6)

Musée Tomo
MUSEUM

7 Map p50, G3

One of Tokyo's most elegant and tasteful museums is named after Kikuchi Tomo, whose collection of contemporary Japanese ceramics wowed them in Washington and London before finally being exhibited at home. Exhibitions change every few months but can be relied on to be atmospheric and beautiful. (智美術館; ☑5733-5131; www.musee-tomo.or.jp; 4-1-35 Toranomon, Minato-ku; adult/student ¥1000/500; ⏰11am-6pm Tue-Sun; Ⓢ Hibiya line to Kamiyachō, exit 4B)

Nogi-jinja
SHINTO SHRINE

8 Map p50, B2

This shrine honours General Nogi Maresuke, a famed commander in the Russo-Japanese War. Hours after Emperor Meiji's funerary procession in 1912, Nogi and his faithful wife committed ritual suicide, following their master into death. An **antiques flea market** is held on the shrine grounds on the fourth Sunday of each month (9am to 4pm). (乃木神社; www.nogijinja.or.jp; 8-11-27 Akasaka, Minato-ku; ⏰9am-5pm; Ⓢ Chiyoda line to Nogizaka, exit 1)

Top Tip
Tokyo Tower View
From Roppongi Crossing, head east on Gaien-higashi-dōri for a view of Tokyo Tower (p52).

Toranomon Hills
LANDMARK

9 Map p50, H2

Opened in June 2014, the 52-storey, 247m Toranomon Hills complex, topped by the Andaz Hotel, is Mori Buildings' latest modification of Tokyo's cityscape. Apart from the hotel, there are pleasant places to eat and drink and a small public garden. (http://toranomonhills.com; 1-23 Toranomon, Minato-ku; Ⓢ Ginza line to Toranomon, exit 1)

Eating

Kikunoi
KAISEKI $$$

10 Map p50, D1

Exquisitely prepared seasonal dishes are as beautiful as they are delicious at this two-Michelin-starred, Tokyo outpost of a three-generation-old Kyoto-based *kaiseki* restaurant. Kikunoi's Chef Murata has written a book translated into English on *kaiseki* (Japanese haute cuisine) that the staff helpfully use to explain the dishes you are served, if you don't speak Japanese. Reservations are necessary. (菊乃井; ☑3568-6055; http://kikunoi.jp; 6-13-8 Akasaka, Minato-ku; lunch/dinner course from ¥5670/8960; ⏰lunch seating noon-1pm, dinner seating 5-8pm; Ⓢ Chiyoda line to Akasaka, exit 7)

Tofuya-Ukai
KAISEKI $$$

11 Map p50, G5

One of Tokyo's most gracious restaurants is located in a former sake brewery (moved from northern Japan),

Understand
Rise of the Megamalls

When Roppongi Hills opened in 2003, it was more than just another shopping mall: it was an ambitious prototype for the future of Tokyo. Developer Mori Minoru envisioned improving the quality of urban life by centralising home, work and leisure into a utopian microcity. Similar projects appeared in succession: Shiodome Shio-site (2004), Tokyo Midtown (2005) and Akasaka Sakas (2008). The newest is Toranomon Hills (2014), another project from Mori Building.

Such developments have proved polarising: conceived during the economic bubble of the late 80s and early 90s and unveiled in harder times, the luxury and exclusivity that they project seem out of step with today's lingering economic malaise. Still, Roppongi Hills is credited with transforming the neighbourhood of Roppongi, once synonymous with sleazy nightlife, into a cultural attraction.

with an exquisite traditional garden, in the shadow of Tokyo Tower. Seasonal preparations of tofu and accompanying dishes are served in the refined *kaiseki* style. Make reservations well in advance. (とうふ屋うかい; ☑3436-1028; www.ukai.co.jp/english/shiba; 4-4-13 Shiba-kōen, Minato-ku; lunch/dinner set menu from ¥5500/8400; ⊗11.30am-10pm, last order 8pm; ☑; Ⓢ Toei Ōedo line to Akabanebashi, exit 8)

Jōmon
IZAKAYA $$

 12 Map p50, D4

This wonderfully cosy kitchen has bar seating, rows of ornate *shochu* (liquor) jugs lining the wall and hundreds of freshly prepared skewers splayed in front of the patrons – don't miss the heavenly *zabuton* beef stick (¥400). It's almost directly across from the Family Mart – look for the name in Japanese on the door. (ジョウモン; ☑3405-2585;

www.teyandei.com/jomon_rop; 5-9-17 Roppongi, Minato-ku; skewers ¥150-1600; ⊗6pm-5am; ☑; Ⓢ Hibiya line to Roppongi, exit 3)

Lauderdale
INTERNATIONAL $$

 13 Map p50, B5

Just off chic Keyaki-zaka and sporting a spacious outdoor terrace, this is an on-trend, all-day dining space that works as well for breakfast as it does for dinner. Weekend brunch is very popular here, particularly the egg dishes. (☑3405-5533; www.lauderdale.co.jp; 6-15-1 Roppongi, Minato-ku; mains from ¥1400; ⊗7am-midnight Mon-Fri, from 8am Sat & Sun; 🛜; Ⓢ Hibiya line to Roppongi, exit 1)

Tsurutontan
NOODLES $

14 Map p50, D4

Huge bowls of udon (thick wheat noodles) are the speciality here. Go for simple (topped with seaweed or pickled plum), exotic (udon carbonara) or filling (Tsuruton *zanmai*: topped with fried tofu, tempura and beef). (つるとんたん; www.tsurutontan.co.jp; 3-14-12 Roppongi, Minato-ku; udon ¥680-1800; 11am-8am; S Hibiya line to Roppongi, exit 5)

Honmura-An
SOBA $$

15 Map p50, C3

This fabled *soba* (buckwheat noodles) shop, once located in Manhattan, now serves its handmade noodles at this minimalist noodle shop on a Roppongi side street. The delicate flavour of these noodles is best appreciated when served on a bamboo mat, with tempura or with dainty slices of *kamo* (duck). (本むら庵; 5772-6657; www.honmuraantokyo.com; 7-14-18 Roppongi, Minato-ku; dishes from ¥1000, set dinner ¥6500; noon-2.30pm & 5.30-10pm Tue-Sun, closed 1st & 3rd Tue of month; S Hibiya line to Roppongi, exit 4)

Gonpachi
IZAKAYA $

16 Map p50, A4

Over the last decade this cavernous old Edo-style space (which inspired a memorable set in Quentin Tarantino's *Kill Bill*) has cemented its rep as a Tokyo dining institution with other less-memorable branches scattered around the city. *Kushiyaki* (charcoal-grilled skewers) are served here alongside noodles, tempura and sushi. (権八; 5771-0170; www.gonpachi.jp/nishi-azabu; 1-13-11 Nishi-Azabu, Minato-ku; skewers ¥180-1500, lunch sets weekday/weekend from ¥800/2050; 11.30am-3.30am; S Hibiya line to Roppongi, exit 2)

Drinking

SuperDeluxe
LOUNGE

17 Map p50, B4

This groovy basement performance space, also a cocktail lounge and club of sorts, stages everything from hula-hoop gatherings to literary evenings and creative presentations in the 20 x 20 PechaKucha (20 slides x 20 seconds) format. Check the website for event details. It's in an unmarked brown-brick building by a shoe-repair shop. (スーパー・デラックス; 5412-0515; www.super-deluxe.com; B1 fl, 3-1-25 Nishi-Azabu, Minato-ku; admission varies; S Hibiya line to Roppongi, exit 1B)

Pink Cow
BAR

18 Map p50, D4

With its animal-print decor, rotating display of local artwork and terrific all-you-can-eat buffet (¥2000) every Friday and Saturday, the Pink Cow is a funky, friendly place to hang out. Also host to stitch-and-bitch evenings, writers' salons and indie-film screenings, it's a good bet if you're in the mood to mix with a creative crowd. (ピンクカウ; www.thepinkcow.com; B1 fl, Roi Bldg, 5-5-1 Roppongi, Minato-ku; 5pm-late Tue-Sun; S Hibiya line to Roppongi, exit 3)

Festa Iikura
KARAOKE

19 Map p50, F4

Kill two *tori* (birds) with one stone and savour some sushi while singing your heart out. Excellent service and complimentary costume rentals make

Display at Japan Sword (p59)

this one of the best places to perfect your rendition of 'My Sharona' – we know you've been practising... (フェスタ飯倉; ☎5570-1500; www.festa-iikura. com; 3-5-7 Azabudai, Minato-ku; 3hr room & meal plan from ¥5000; ◷5pm-5am Mon-Sat; **S**Hibiya line to Kamiyachō, exit 2)

Agave
BAR

20 🍷 Map p50, C4

Rawhide chairs, *cruzas de rosas* (crosses decorated with roses) and tequila shots for the willing make Agave a good place for a long night in search of the sacred worm. Luckily, this gem in the jungle that is Roppongi is more about savouring the subtleties of its 400-plus varieties of tequila than tossing back shots of Cuervo. (アガヴェ; ☎3497-0229; www.agave.jp; B1 fl, 7-15-10 Roppongi, Minato-ku; ◷6.30pm-2am Mon-Thu, to 4am Fri & Sat; **S**Hibiya or Ōedo line to Roppongi, exit 2)

Muse
CLUB

21 🍷 Map p50, A5

This catacomb-like underground club, with intimate booths, dance floors and

billiards, has an excellent mix of locals and foreigners. There's something for everyone here, whether you want to dance up a storm or just feel like playing darts or table tennis. (ミューズ; ☎5467-1188; www.muse-web.com; B1 fl, 4-1-1 Nishi-Azabu, Minato-ku; admission women/ men incl 2 drinks free/¥3000; ◷9pm-late Mon-Fri, from 10pm Sat & Sun; **S**Hibiya line to Roppongi, exit 3)

Janome
CAFE, BAR

22 🍷 Map p50, H3

Janome is the base for the 'Little Tokyo' project, which combines a quirky cool cafe, bar, gallery and design shop with an events space. With free wi-fi, it's a great hang-out in an area that, thanks to the adjacent Toronomon Hills development, is on the up and up. (ジャノメ; http://littletyo. com; 1-2-1 Atago, Minato-ku; ◷8.30am-11pm Mon-Fri, noon-6pm Sat; **S**Hibiya line to Kamiyachō, exit 3; 🛜)

MARTIN MOOS/GETTY IMAGES ©

Local Life
Nishi-Azabu

A world away from brash Roppongi (but just down the road), Nishi-Azabu is the sophisticated haunt of Tokyo's rich and famous. Many bars have a members-only policy, but fortunately not **These** (Map p50, A4; テーゼ; ☑5466-7331; www.these-jp.com; 2-15-12 Nishi-Azabu, Minato-ku; cover charge ¥500; ⊘7pm-4am, to 2am Sun; ⑤Hibiya line to Roppongi, exit 3). Nicknamed the 'library bar' (and pronounced tay-zay), These is full of nooks and crannies, cosy sofas and, yes, books. Look for the torches out front; reservations recommended.

Salsa Sudada   DANCE
23 ◉ Map p50, C3

Tokyo's salsa fanatics come here to mingle and merengue. If you don't know how to dance, they'll teach you (1½-hour lessons held nightly; ¥1500). (サルサスダーダ; www.salsasudada.org; 3rd fl, Fusion Bldg, 7-13-8 Roppongi, Minato-ku; Fri & Sat ¥2000, Sun-Thu free; ⊘6pm-2am; ⑱Hibiya line to Roppongi, exit 4B)

Entertainment

National Theatre   THEATRE
24 ✪ Map p50, G1

This is the capital's premier venue for traditional performing arts with a 1600-seat and a 590-seat auditorium. Performances include kabuki, *gagaku* (music of the imperial court) and bunraku (classic puppet theatre). Earphones with English translation are available for hire (¥650 plus ¥1000 deposit). Check the website for performance schedules. (国立劇場; ☑3265-7411; www.ntj.jac.go.jp/english; 4-1 Hayabusa-chō, Chiyoda-ku; tickets from ¥1500; ⑤Hanzōmon line to Hanzōmon, exit 1)

STB 139   JAZZ
25 ✪ Map p50, C4

A large, lovely space that draws big-name domestic and international jazz acts running the gamut of the genre; check the website for the current line-up. This classy joint is also a good place to have an Italian dinner before a show; call for reservations between 11am and 8pm Monday to Saturday. (スイートベイジル; ☑5474-1395; http://stb139.co.jp; 6-7-11 Roppongi, Minato-ku; admission ¥3000-7000; ⊘6-11pm Mon-Sat; ⑤Hibiya line to Roppongi, exit 3)

Kingyo   CABARET
26 ✪ Map p50, D4

Next to a cemetery off Roppongi's main drag, cheeky Kingyo puts on a glitzy, colourful and sexually tame cabaret of pretty boys, glammed-up *nyū hāfu* (transsexual) and drag-queen performers. There are a couple of shows each night, and you'll be expected to buy drinks and snacks on top of admission. (金魚; ☑3478-3000; www.kingyo.co.jp; 3-14-17 Roppongi, Minato-ku; admission from ¥3500; ⊘shows 7.30pm & 10pm Tue-Sun; ⑤Hibiya line to Roppongi, exit 3)

Shopping

Japan Traditional Crafts Aoyama Square
CRAFTS

27 🔒 Map p50, B1

Supported by the Japanese Ministry of Economy, Trade and Industry, this is as much a showroom as a shop exhibiting a broad range of traditional crafts, including lacquerwork boxes, woodwork, cut glass, paper, textiles and earthy pottery. The emphasis is on high-end pieces, but you can find beautiful things in all prices ranges here. (伝統工芸 青山スクエア; http://kougeihin.jp/home.shtml; 8-1-22 Akasaka, Minato-ku; ⏰11am-7pm, Mon-Sun except New Year's holidays; Ⓢ Ginza line to Aoyama-itchōme, exit 4)

Tolman Collection
ARTS, CRAFTS

28 🔒 Map p50, H5

Based in a traditional wooden building, this reputable gallery represents nearly 50 leading Japanese artists of printing, lithography, etching, woodblock and more. Quality prints start at around ¥10,000 and rise steeply from there. From Daimon Station, walk west towards Zōjō-ji temple and turn left at the shop Create. You'll soon see the gallery on your left. (トールマンコレクション; ☎3434-1300; www.tolmantokyo.com; 2-2-18 Shiba-Daimon, Minato-ku; ⏰11am-7pm Wed-Mon; Ⓢ Ōedo line to Daimon, exit A3)

Souvenir From Tokyo
SOUVENIRS

An expert selection of homegrown design bits and bobs that make for perfect, unique souvenirs: a mobile by Tempo, zig-zag tote from Mint Designs or a set of cheeky tea cups from Amabro, for example. It's in the basement of the National Art Center Tokyo (see 6 Ⓖ Map p50, B3). (スーベニアフロムトーキョー; www.souvenirfromtokyo.jp; Basement fl, National Art Center Tokyo, 7-22-2 Roppongi, Minato-ku; ⏰10am-6pm Sat-Mon, Wed & Thu, to 8pm Fri; Ⓢ Chiyoda line to Nogizaka, exit 6)

Japan Sword
ANTIQUES

29 🔒 Map p50, H2

If you're after a samurai sword or weaponry, this venerable place sells the genuine article – including antique sword guards and samurai helmets dating from the Edo period – as well as convincing replicas crafted by hand. Be sure to enquire about export and transport restrictions. (日本刀剣; ☎3434-4324; www.japansword.co.jp; 3-8-1 Toranomon, Minato-ku; ⏰9.30am-6pm Mon-Fri, to 5pm Sat; Ⓢ Ginza line to Toranomon, exit 2)

☑ Top Tip

Play It Safe

Pickpocketing is rare in Tokyo, but if it is going to happen, it will happen in Roppongi. Note that shadier bars have been known to overcharge credit cards; drink spiking has also been reported. Be particularly wary of places that employ street touts.

Explore

Ebisu & Meguro

Ebisu – named for the beer Yebisu that was once brewed here – and Meguro represent Tokyo on a more human scale. There's a smattering of small but significant museums, such as the Tokyo Metropolitan Museum of Photography, plus excellent restaurants and bars. Nearby, the fashionable residential neighbourhoods Daikanyama and Naka-Meguro are resplendent with stylish boutiques and cafes.

The Sights in a Day

 Start the day in Ebisu and spend the morning at Yebisu Garden Place (follow the 'Skywalk' from the east exit), taking in an exhibition at the **Tokyo Metropolitan Museum of Photography** (p65; closed for renovation until August 2016) and touring the **Beer Museum Yebisu** (p65). Then join the local office workers in the queue at **Afuri** (p67) for a bowl of *rāmen* (soup and noodles with a sprinkling of meat and vegetables).

After lunch, take the JR Yamanote line one stop from Ebisu to Meguro and visit the **Institute for Nature Study** (p65) and **Tokyo Metropolitan Teien Art Museum** (p65). Next head down Meguro-dōri to the quirky **Meguro Parasitological Museum** (p66) and then continue along the wide boulevard, also known as Tokyo's design district, to check out the shops that make up the **Meguro Interior Shops Community** (p68).

Take a bus back to Meguro station and have dinner at legendary *tonkatsu* (deep-fried pork cutlet) shop **Tonki** (p66). Then take the train back to Ebisu and hit that neighbourhood's lively bar scene, starting at **Buri** (p68).

For a local's day in Daikanyama & Naka-Meguro, see p62.

Local Life

Shopping in Daikanyama & Naka-Meguro (p62)

Best of Tokyo

Parks & Gardens
Institute for Nature Study (p65)

Galleries & Museums
Tokyo Metropolitan Museum of Photography (p65)

Eating
Tonki (p66)

Afuri (p67)

Shopping
Meguro Interior Shops Community (p68)

Nightlife & Live Music
Buri (p68)

Getting There

🚃 **Train** The JR Yamanote line stops at Ebisu and Meguro. The Tōkyu-Tōyoko line runs from Shibuya to Daikanyama and Naka-Meguro.

Ⓢ **Subway** The Fukutoshin line continues on the Tōkyu-Tōyoko line after Shibuya; the Hibiya line stops at Ebisu and Naka-Meguro; the Namboku and Mita lines stop at Meguro and Shirokanedai.

Local Life
Shopping in Daikanyama & Naka-Meguro

Just one stop from Shibuya, but a world away, Daikanyama is an upscale residential enclave with pavement cafes, fashionable boutiques and an unhurried pace. Neighbouring Naka-Meguro is Daikanyama's bohemian little sister, home to secondhand shops and secret lounge bars. At the heart of the neighbourhood is the Meguro-gawa, a canal with a leafy promenade.

❶ Kooky Boutiques

Just because Daikanyama is wealthy, doesn't mean it's uptight. In fact, some of Tokyo's most out-there boutiques are right here. Like **Harcoza** (ハルコ座; www.harcoza.com; 2-15-9 Ebisu-Nishi, Shibuya-ku; 🕑11am-7pm Wed-Mon; 🚃Tōkyū Tōyoko line to Daikanyama, north exit), which specialises in candy-coloured clothing and accessories with a DIY art-school vibe.

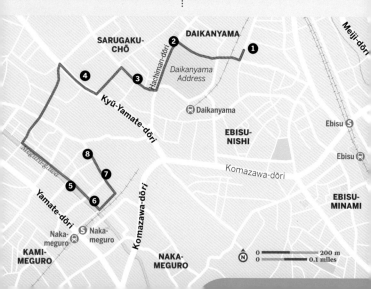

❷ Japanese Designers

Lots of home-grown designers have their flagship stores here too, like Tsumori Chisato and Sunao Kuwahara, who have shops in the **La Fuente Building** (ラ・フエンテ; 11-1 Sarugakuchō, Shibuya-ku; ⏰11am-8pm; 🚇Tōkyū Tōyoko line to Daikanyama, main exit). Other local brands to keep an eye out for: Frapbois and Mercibeaucoup.

❸ Traditional Meets Modern

Surrounded by trendy boutiques, **Okura** (オクラ; 20-11 Sarugaku-chō, Shibuya-ku; ⏰11.30am-8pm, 11am-8.30pm Sat & Sun; 🚇Tōkyū Tōyoko line to Daikanyama) offers something different: wardrobe staples (jeans, T-shirts, work shirts) dyed in traditional indigo. The building is unique too – it looks like a farmhouse.

❹ Book-Lovers' Paradise

Locals love **Daikanyama T-Site** (代官山T-SITE; http://tsite.jp/daikanyama; 17-5 Sarugaku-chō, Shibuya-ku; ⏰7am-2am; 🚇Tōkyū Tōyoko line to Daikanyama). This stylish shrine to the printed word has a fantastic collection of books on travel, art, design and food (some in English). Plus you can sit at the in-house Starbucks and read all afternoon – if you can get a seat.

❺ A Leafy Stroll

Lined with cherry trees and a walking path, the **Meguro-gawa** (not so much a river as a canal) is what gives Naka-Meguro its unlikely village vibe. On either side you'll find all manner of quirky boutiques, plus cafes, like

Hanabi (2-16-11 Aobadai, Meguro-ku; dishes around ¥800; ⏰11.30am-midnight; 🚇Hibiya line to Naka-Meguro), overlooking the water, a few blocks to the west when you reach the river.

❻ Treasure Hunting

A perfect example of one of Naka-Meguro's tiny, impeccably curated boutiques, **Vase** (1-7-7 Kami-Meguro, Meguro-ku; ⏰noon-8pm; 🚇Hibiya line to Naka-Meguro) stocks cutting-edge designers and a few vintage pieces (for men and women). It's in a little white house set back from the Meguro-gawa (with the name on the post box).

❼ Hidden Art

Quite possibly the city's tiniest art gallery, **The Container** (http://the-container.com; 1-8-30 Kami-Meguro, Meguro-ku; ⏰11am-9pm Wed-Mon, to 8pm Sat & Sun; 🚇Hibiya line to Naka-Meguro) is literally a shipping container located within a hair salon. Really, it doesn't get much more Tokyo than that. Installations feature contemporary artists, both Japanese and international.

❽ Drinks with Bikes

Sip a cocktail at **Kinfolk** (キンフォーク; ☎5499-8683; www.kinfolklife.com/tokyo; 2nd fl, 1-11-1 Kami-Meguro, Meguro-ku; ⏰6pm-midnight; 🚇Hibiya line to Naka-Meguro), a dim, moody lounge run by the custom-bicycle makers of the same name. It's in an old house with the ceiling cut away to expose the wooden rafters above; the entrance is up a rickety metal staircase above a restaurant.

SARUGAKU-CHŌ

DAIKANYAMA

HIRO-O

SHIBUYA-KU

15

Meiji-dōri

Hachiman-dōri

Shibuya-gawa

Komazawa-dōri

Yamatane Museum of Art

5

400 m
0.2 miles

Daikanyama Address

Kyū-Yamate-dōri

16

Ebisu-yokochō

18

Ebisu Prime Square Plaza

8

Meiji-dōri

EBISU

17

Daikanyama

EBISU-NISHI

13

Ebisu

Ebisu

11

Komazawa-dōri

10

Komazawa-dōri

14

Naka-meguro

NAKA-MEGURO

EBISU-MINAMI

19

Sky Walk

Beer Museum Yebisu

Yebisu Garden Place

2

Platanus-dōri

Shuto Expwy No 2

1

Tokyo Metropolitan Museum of Photography

Kusunoki-dōri

Yamate-dōri

Chaya-zaka (Slope)

MITA

Meguro-gawa

Shizen Kyōiku-en

Tokyo Metropolitan Teien Art Museum

3

Institute for Nature Study

MEGURO

9

Meguro

Meguro

SHINAGAWA-KU

MEGURO-KU

12

6

Meguro Parasitological Museum

Gonnosuke-zaka

7

Meguro-dōri

SHIMO-MEGURO

KAMI-ŌSAKI

For reviews see

⊙	Sights	p65
⊗	Eating	p66
⊖	Drinking	p68
✪	Entertainment	p69
🔒	Shopping	p69

Sights

Tokyo Metropolitan Museum of Photography

MUSEUM

1 ◉ Map p64, C3

Tokyo's principal photography museum is closed through August 2016 for renovations. In addition to drawing on its extensive collection, the museum also hosts travelling shows (usually several exhibitions happen simultaneously; ticket prices depend on how many you see). The museum is at the far end of Yebisu Garden Place, on the right side if you're coming from Ebisu Station. (東京都写真美術館; ☑3280-0099; www.syabi.com; 1-13-3 Mita, Meguro-ku; admission ¥600-1650; ☑10am-6pm Tue, Wed, Sat & Sun, to 8pm Thu & Fri; ☒JR Yamanote line to Ebisu, east exit)

Beer Museum Yebisu

MUSEUM

2 ◉ Map p64, C3

Photos, vintage bottles and posters document the rise of Yebisu, and beer in general, in Japan at this small museum located where the actual Yebisu brewery stood until 1988. At the 'tasting salon' you can sample four kinds of Yebisu beer (¥400 each). It's behind the Mitsukoshi department store at Yebisu Garden Place. (エビスビール記念館; ☑5423-7255; www.sapporoholdings.jp/english/guide/yebisu; 4-20-1 Ebisu, Shibuya-ku; admission free; ☑11am-7pm Tue-Sun; ☒JR Yamanote line to Ebisu, east exit)

Tokyo Metropolitan Teien Art Museum

MUSEUM

3 ◉ Map p64, D4

Although the Teien museum hosts regular art exhibitions – usually of decorative arts – its appeal lies principally in the building itself: it's an art deco structure, a former princely estate built in 1933, designed by French architect Henri Rapin. The museum reopened in late 2014 after a lengthy renovation and now includes a modern annex designed by artist Sugimoto Hiroshi. (東京都庭園美術館; www.teien-art-museum.ne.jp; 5-21-9 Shirokanedai, Minato-ku; admission varies; ☑10am-6pm, closed 2nd & 4th Wed each month; ☒JR Yamanote line to Meguro, east exit)

Institute for Nature Study

PARK

4 ◉ Map p64, D4

What would Tokyo look like left to its own natural devices? Since 1949 this park, affiliated with the Tokyo National Museum, has let the local flora go wild. There are wonderful walks through its forests, marshes and ponds. No more than 300 people are allowed in at a time, which makes for an even more peaceful setting. (自然教育園, Shizen Kyōiku-en; ☑3441-7176; www.ins.kahaku.go.jp; 5-21-5 Shirokanedai, Meguro-ku; adult/child ¥310/free; ☑9am-4.30pm Tue-Sun Sep-Apr, to 5pm Tue-Sun May-Aug, last entry 4pm; ☒JR Yamanote line to Meguro, east exit)

Yamatane Museum of Art

MUSEUM

5 Map p64, C1

When Western ideas entered Japan following the Meiji Restoration (1868), many artists set out to master oil and canvas. Others poured new energy into *nihonga* – Japanese style painting, usually done with mineral pigments on silk or paper – and the masters are represented here. From the collection of 1800 works, a small number are displayed in thematic exhibitions. (山種美術館; ☎5777-8600; www.yamatane-museum.or.jp; 3-12-36 Hiroo, Shibuya-ku; adult/student/child ¥1000/800/free, special exhibits extra; ⊙10am-5pm Tue-Sun; ☒JR Yamanote line to Ebisu, west exit)

☑ Top Tip

Meguro-dōri Buses

Buses 2 and 7, departing from outside Meguro Station, run down Meguro-dōri, stopping at Otori-jinja-mae – the closest stop for the Meguro Parasitological Museum and also the starting point for the Meguro Interior Shops Community (p68). At any point along Meguro-dōri you can catch a bus heading back to Meguro Station. A single ride costs ¥210. Drop your coins in the slot next to the driver (or swipe your Suica card); exit through the rear doors.

Meguro Parasitological Museum

MUSEUM

6 Map p64, B5

Here's one for fans of the grotesque: this small museum was established in 1953 by a local doctor concerned by the increasing number of parasites he was encountering due to unsanitary postwar conditions. The grisly centrepiece is an 8.8m-long tapeworm found in the body of a 40-year-old Yokohama man. (目黒寄生虫館; ☎3716-1264; http://kiseichu.org; 4-1-1 Shimo-Meguro, Meguro-ku; admission free; ⊙10am-5pm Tue-Sun; ☒2 or 7 from Meguro Station to Ōtori-jinja-mae, ☒JR Yamanote line to Meguro, west exit)

Take a Break Octopus-dumpling stand Ganko Dako is across the street.

Eating

Tonki

TONKATSU $

7 Map p64, C5

One of Tokyo's best *tonkatsu* (crumbed pork cutlets) restaurants, Tonki has a loyal following. The seats at the counter – where you can watch the perfectly choreographed chefs – are the most coveted. From the station, walk down Meguro-dōri, take a left at the first alley and look for a white sign and *noren* (doorway curtains) across the sliding doors. (とんき; 1-2-1 Shimo-Meguro, Meguro-ku; meals ¥1900; ⊙4-10.45pm Wed-Mon, closed 3rd Mon of month; ☒JR Yamanote line to Meguro, west exit)

Afuri

RĀMEN **$**

8 Map p64, C2

Hardly your typical, surly *rāmen-ya*, Afuri has upbeat young cooks and a hip industrial interior. The unorthodox menu might draw eye-rolls from purists, but house specialities such as *yuzu-shio* (a light, salty broth flavoured with *yuzu*, a type of citrus) draw lines at lunchtime. Order from the vending machine. (あふり; 1-1-7 Ebisu, Shibuya-ku; noodles from ¥750; ⏱11am-5am; 🚇JR Yamanote line to Ebisu, east exit)

Beard

BISTRO **$$**

9 Map p64, C4

One of Tokyo's hottest new restaurants, Beard serves up casual, creative bistro fare inspired by the peripatetic chef's travels. It's a small place, so reservations are recommended. Sunday brunch, featuring dense ricotta hot cakes (¥1200), is popular too; bookings aren't accepted for brunch, so turn up early or just before closing. (☎5496-0567; http://b-e-a-r-d.com; 1-17-22 Meguro, Meguro-ku; mains from ¥1700; ⏱5.30-10.30pm Tue-Sat, 10am-1.30pm Sun; 🚇JR Yamanote line to Meguro, west exit)

Ippo

IZAKAYA **$$**

10 Map p64, C2

This mellow little *izakaya* (Japanese pub-eatery) specialises in simple pleasures: fish and sake (there's an English sign out front that says just that). The friendly chefs speak some English and can help you decide what

to have grilled, steamed, simmered or fried. The entrance is up the wooden stairs. (一歩; ☎3445-8418; 2nd fl, 1-22-10 Ebisu, Shibuya-ku; dishes ¥500-1500; ⏱6pm-3am; 🚇JR Yamanote line to Ebisu, east exit)

Ouca

ICE CREAM **$**

11 Map p64, C2

Green tea isn't the only flavour Japan has contributed to the ice-cream playbook; other delicious innovations available at Ouca include *kuro-goma* (black sesame) and *beni imo* (purple sweet potato). (櫻花; www.ice-ouca.com; 1-6-6 Ebisu, Shibuya-ku; ice creams from ¥390; ⏱11am-11.30pm Mar-Oct, noon-11pm Nov-Feb; 🚇JR Yamanote line to Ebisu, east exit)

Ganko Dako

STREET FOOD **$**

12 Map p64, B5

This street stall dishes out steaming hot *tako-yaki* (grilled octopus dumplings). It's located, unfortunately, across from the Meguro Parasitological Museum; nonetheless, Ganko Dako draws people in – check out the celebrity signings on the wall. (頑固蛸; 3-11-6 Meguro, Meguro-ku; 6 for ¥500; ⏱11am-1am; 🚃JR Yamanote line to Meguro, west exit)

Drinking

Buri   BAR

13 🚇 Map p64, B2

Buri – the name means 'super' in Hiroshima dialect – is one of Ebisu's most popular *tachinomi-ya* (standing bars). On almost any night you can find a lively crowd packed in around the horseshoe-shaped counter here. Generous quantities of sake (over 50 varieties; ¥750) are served semifrozen, like slushies in colourful jars. (ぶり; ☏3496-7744; 1-14-1 Ebisu-nishi, Shibuya-ku; ⏱5pm-3am; 🚃JR Yamanote line to Ebisu, west exit)

Nakame Takkyū Lounge   LOUNGE

14 🚇 Map p64, A3

Takkyū means table tennis and it's a serious sport in Japan. This hilarious bar looks like a university table-tennis clubhouse – right down to the tatty furniture and posters of star players on the wall. It's in an apartment building next to a parking garage (go all the way down the corridor past the bikes); ring the doorbell for entry. (中目卓球ラウンジ; 2nd fl, Lion House Naka-Meguro, 1-3-13 Kami-Meguro, Meguro-ku; cover before/after 10pm ¥500/800; ⏱7pm-2am Mon-Sat; 🚇Hibiya line to Naka-Meguro)

Air   CLUB

15 🚇 Map p64, B1

DJs spin mostly house and techno here, and the sound system is top of the line. Expect a good night out on any Friday or Saturday night. Keep an eye out for Frames (フレイムス) – the entrance to the basement club is inside. Bring your ID. (エアー; www.air-tokyo.com; Basement, Hikawa Bldg, 2-11 Sarugaku-chō, Shibuya-ku; cover from ¥2500; ⏱from 10pm Thu-Tue; 🚃Tōkyū Tōyoko line to Daikanyama)

Enjoy House   BAR

16 🚇 Map p64, B2

Decked out with velveteen booths, fairy lights and foliage, Enjoy House is a deeply funky place to spend the evening. DJs spin regularly, but

Local Life
Meguro Interior Shops Community

There are dozens of homewares shops stretched out along 3km of Meguro-dōri – otherwise known as **Meguro Interior Shops Community** (ミスク, MISC; Map p64, A5; http://misc.co.jp/; Meguro-dōri; 🚃JR Yamanote line to Meguro, west exit). Wares include modernist wonders, high kitsch, antiques and everything in between. Note that many stores close on Wednesdays.

there's still no cover charge. By day it's a burger shop. Look for the name painted in red letters in English on the 2nd-floor window. (http://enjoyhouse.jugem.jp; 2nd fl, 2-9-9 Ebisu-nishi, Shibuya-ku; drinks from ¥600; ☉noon-late; ℝJR Yamanote line to Ebisu, west exit)

Entertainment

Unit
LIVE MUSIC

17 ⭐ Map p64, A2

On weekends, this subterranean club has two shows: live music in the evening and a DJ-hosted event after hours. Acts range from Japanese indie bands to overseas artists making their Japanese debut. Unit is less grungy than other Tokyo live houses; it draws a stylish young crowd and, thanks to its high ceilings, it doesn't get too smoky. (ユニット; ♪5459-8630; www.unit-tokyo.com; 1-34-17 Ebisu-nishi, Shibuya-ku; ¥2500-5000; ℝTōkyū Tōyoko line to Daikanyama)

Liquid Room
LIVE MUSIC

18 ⭐ Map p64, C2

When this storied concert hall moved to Ebisu from seedy Kabukichō it cleaned up its act, but Liquid Room is still a great place to catch big-name acts in an intimate setting. Both Japanese and international bands play here, and every once in a while there's an all-night gig. Tickets sell out fast. (リキッドルーム; ♪5464-0800; www.liquidroom.net; 3-16-6 Higashi, Shibuya-ku; ℝJR Yamanote line to Ebisu, west exit)

Institute for Nature Study (p65)

Shopping

Kapital
FASHION

19 🔒 Map p64, B3

One of Japan's hottest brands, Kapital is a world away from Tokyo's pop image. The label is known for its premium denim, dyed a dozen times the traditional way, earthy knits and lushly patterned scarves. (キャピタル; ♪5725-3923; http://kapital.jp; 2-20-2 Ebisu, Shibuya-ku; ☉11am-8pm; ℝJR Yamanote line to Ebisu, west exit)

Explore

Shibuya

Shibuya hits you over the head with its sheer presence: its omnipresent flow of people, glowing video screens and pure exuberence. This is the beating heart of Tokyo's youth culture, where the fashion is loud, the street culture vivid and the nightclubs run until dawn. Nowhere else says 'Welcome to Tokyo' better than this, and the neighbourhood is a must-see for anyone interested in Tokyo pop culture.

The Sights in a Day

☼ Before even leaving Shibuya Station, check out the mural **Myth of Tomorrow** (p74). Then head out to pay your respects to the loyal dog, **Hachikō** (p74). That's **Shibuya Crossing** (p74) just in front of the station plaza (be sure to return here at night, to see it all lit up). To the east is the new **Shibuya Hikarie** (p75) building, with galleries on the 8th floor and views over the neighbourhood from the 11th floor. Round out your visit there with lunch at **d47 Shokudō** (p75) on the 8th floor.

☼ In the afternoon explore the neighbourhood's central drag, **Center-gai** (p74). There are several worthwhile shops around here, including **Tōkyū Hands** (p78). Take a peek into teen-fashion trend machine **Shibuya 109** (p78) and memorialise your visit with a stop at **Purikura no Mecca** (p74).

☾ For dinner, feast on top-grade sukiyaki at **Matsukiya** (p76) or fresh seafood at **Kaikaya** (p76). Check in with Tokyo's craft-beer scene at **Good Beer Faucets** (p77). Then, if you've got energy in reserve, hit nightclub **Womb** (p77) and dance until the trains start running again at dawn.

 Best of Tokyo

Food
d47 Shokudō (p75)

Matsukiya (p76)

Sushi-no-Midori (p76)

Shopping & Markets
Tōkyū Hands (p78)

Fake Tokyo (p78)

Nightlife & Music
Womb (p77)

WWW (p78)

Nonbei-yokochō (p77)

Pop Culture
Shibuya Crossing (p74)

Purikura no Mecca (p74)

Shibuya 109 (p78)

Getting There

🚈 **Train** The JR Yamanote, Tōkyū Tōyōko and Keiō Inokashira lines stop at Shibuya.

Ⓢ **Subway** The Ginza, Hanzōmon and Fukutoshin lines all stop at Shibuya.

A **B** **C** **D**

1

KAMIYAMA-CHŌ

NHK Broadcast Center & Studio Park

JINNAN

Inokashira-dōri

Kamiyama Shōtengai

Kōen-dōri

UDAGAWA-CHŌ

2

SHŌTŌ

20

23

18

19 Shibuya Center-gai

24

21

3

14 Bunkamura-dōri

13

4 Shibuya Center-gai

5

Purikura no Mecca

22

Shibuya Crossing

1

Hachikō Statue

3

4

DŌGENZAKA

16

15

Keiō Shibuya

12

Shibuya Mark City

11

5

MARUYAMA-CHŌ

9

10

Dōgenzaka

Tamagawa-dōri

Shuto Expwy No 3

Cerulean Tower Tōkyū Hotel

Map labels:
- 0 / 200 m
- 0 / 0.1 miles
- Meiji-dōri
- KITA-AOYAMA
- United Nations University
- 17
- Jingo-dōri
- Miyashita-kōen
- Mitake-kōen
- SHIBUYA-KU
- Nonbei-yokochō
- Ⓢ Shibuya
- Miyamasu-zaka
- Aoyama-dōri
- 7 6 Shibuya Hikarie
- 8 d47 Museum
- Shibuya
- East Exit Bus Terminal
- 2
- West Exit Bus Terminal
- Myth of Tomorrow
- Tōkyū Shibuya
- Shibuya-gawa
- Meiji-dōri

Sights

Shibuya Crossing
STREET

1 ◉ Map p72, D4

Rumoured to be the world's busiest, this intersection in front of Shibuya Station is famously known as 'The Scramble'. It's an awesome spectacle of giant video screens and neon, guaranteed to give you a 'Wow – I'm in Tokyo!' feeling. People come from all directions at once – sometimes over a thousand with every light change – yet still manage to dodge each other with a practiced, nonchalant agility. (渋谷スクランブル交差点, Shibuya Scramble; 🚉JR Yamanote line to Shibuya, Hachikō exit)

Myth of Tomorrow
PUBLIC ART

2 ◉ Map p72, E4

Okamoto Tarō's mural, *Myth of Tomorrow* (1967), was commissioned by a Mexican luxury hotel but went missing two years later. It finally turned up in 2003 and, in 2008, the haunting 30m-long work, which depicts the atomic bomb exploding over Hiroshima, was installed inside Shibuya Station. It's on the 2nd floor, on the way to the Inokashira line. (明日の神話, Asu no Shinwa; 🚉JR Yamanote line to Shibuya, Hachikō exit)

Hachikō Statue
STATUE

3 ◉ Map p72, D4

Come meet Tokyo's most famous pooch, Hachikō. This Akita dog came to Shibuya Station every day to meet his master, a professor, returning from work. The professor died in 1925, but Hachikō kept coming to the station until his own death 10 years later. The story became legend and a small statue was erected in the dog's memory in front of Shibuya Station. (ハチ公像; Hachikō Plaza; 🚉JR Yamanote line to Shibuya, Hachikō exit)

Shibuya Center-gai
STREET

4 ◉ Map p72, D3

Shibuya's main drag is closed to cars and chock-a-block with fast-food joints and high-street fashion shops. At night, lit bright as day, with a dozen competing soundtracks (coming from who knows where), wares spilling onto the streets, shady touts in sunglasses, and strutting teens, it feels like a block party – or Tokyo's version of a classic Asian night market. (渋谷センター街; Shibuya Sentā-gai; 🚉JR Yamanote line to Shibuya, Hachikō exit)

Purikura no Mecca
ARCADE

5 ◉ Map p72, D3

It's easy to see why teens get sucked into the cult of *purikura* ('print club', aka photo booths): the digitally enhanced photos automatically airbrush away blemishes and add doe eyes and long lashes for good measure (so you look like an anime version of yourself). After primping and posing, decorate the images on screen with touch pens. (プリクラのメッカ; 1-23-10 Jinnan, Shibuya-ku; purikura ¥400; 🕔10am-9pm; 🚉JR Yamanote line to Shibuya, Hachikō exit)

Shibuya Hikarie

BUILDING

6 Map p72, F4

This glistening 34-storey tower, which opened in 2012, is just the first step in what promises to be a massive redesign of Shibuya. Sandwiched between the shops on the lower floors and the offices on the upper floors are a couple of worthwhile cultural sights on the 8th floor. (渋谷ヒカリエ; ☎5468-5892; www.hikarie.jp; 2-21-1 Shibuya, Shibuya-ku; ☒JR Yamanote line to Shibuya, east exit)

d47 Museum

MUSEUM

7 Map p72, F4

Lifestyle brand D&D Department combs the country for the platonic ideals of the utterly ordinary: the perfect broom, bottle opener or salt shaker (to name a few examples). See rotating exhibitions of its latest finds from all 47 prefectures in this one-room museum. The excellent d47 Design Travel shop is next door. (www.hikarie8.com/d47museum; 8th fl, Hikarie Bldg, 2-21-1 Shibuya, Shibuya-ku; admission free; ◷11am-8pm; ☒JR Yamanote line to Shibuya, east exit)

Take a Break Grab lunch at sister restaurant d47 Shokudō.

Eating

d47 Shokudō

JAPANESE $

8 Map p72, F4

There are 47 prefectures in Japan and d47 serves a changing line-up of *teishoku* (set meals) that evoke the specialities of each, from the fermented tofu of Okinawa to the stuffed squid of Hokkaido. A larger menu of small plates is available in the evening. Picture windows offer bird's-eye views over the trains coming and going at Shibuya Station. (d47食堂; www.hikarie8.com/d47shokudo/about.shtml; 8th fl, Shibuya Hikarie, 2-21-1 Shibuya, Shibuya-ku; meals ¥1100-1680; ◷11am-2.30pm & 6-11pm; ☒JR Yamanote line to Shibuya, east exit)

Understand

Love Hotels

Sky-high residential rents mean many young people live at home until marriage; consequently, *rabuho* ('love hotels' for amorous encounters) have become a crucial part of modern courtship rituals. They're notorious for their fantastical decor – intended to evoke distant palaces or exotic islands.

Shibuya's **Dōgenzaka** (道玄坂, Love Hotel Hill; ☒JR Yamanote line to Shibuya, Hachikō exit) has one of the largest collections of love hotels in the city. If you're travelling as a couple, a *rabuho* can be a cheap alternative to a business hotel: an all-night 'stay' starts around ¥6000 (a three-hour daytime 'rest' costs about ¥4000).

Matsukiya

SUKIYAKI $$$

9 ✗ Map p72, B5

Matsukiya has been making *sukiyaki* (thinly sliced beef, simmered and then dipped in raw egg) since 1890 and they really, really know what they're doing. It's worth upgrading to the premium course (¥7350) for even meltier meat, cooked to perfection at your table. There's a white sign out front and the entrance is up some stairs. Reservations are recommended. (松木家; ☎3461-2651; 6-8 Maruyama-chō, Shibuya-ku; sukiyaki from ¥5250; ⏰11.30am-1.30pm & 5-11pm Mon-Sat; ⎘JR Yamanote line to Shibuya, Hachikō exit)

Sushi-no-Midori

SUSHI $$

11 ✗ Map p72, C4

Locally famous for its generous, exceedingly reasonable sushi sets, Sushi-no-Midori almost always has a line. Take a number from the ticket machine (and, if the line is long, head out for a little shopping). It's least crowded around 3pm on weekdays. (寿司の美登利; www.sushinomidori.co.jp; 4th fl, Mark City, 1-12-3 Dōgenzaka, Shibuya-ku; meals ¥800-2800; ⏰11am-10pm; ⎘JR Yamanote line to Shibuya, Hachikō exit)

Kaikaya

SEAFOOD $$

10 ✗ Map p72, A5

Kaikaya is one chef's attempt to bring the beach to Shibuya. Most everything on the menu is caught in nearby Sagami Bay, and the super-fresh seafood is served both Japanese- and Western-style. One must-try is *maguro no kama* (tuna collar). Kaikaya is a boisterous, popular place; reservations are recommended. (開花屋; ☎3770-0878; www.kaikaya.com; 23-7 Maruyama-chō, Shibuya-ku; lunch from ¥780, dishes ¥680-2300; ⏰11.30am-2pm & 5.30-11.30pm Mon-Fri, 5.30-11.30pm Sat & Sun; ⎘JR Yamanote line to Shibuya, Hachikō exit)

Food Show

SUPERMARKET $

12 ✗ Map p72, D4

This take-away paradise in the basement of Shibuya Station has steamers of dumplings, crisp *karaage* (Japanese-style fried chicken), heaps of salads and cakes almost too pretty to eat. Look for discount stickers on *bentō* (boxed meals) and sushi sets after 5pm. A green sign pointing downstairs marks the entrance at Hachikō Plaza. (フードショー; Basement, 2-24-1 Shibuya, Shibuya-ku; ⏰10am-9pm; ✐; ⎘JR Yamanote line to Shibuya, Hachikō exit)

Sagatani

SOBA $

13 ✗ Map p72, C3

Proving that Tokyo is only expensive to those who don't know better, this all-night joint serves up bamboo steamers of delicious noodles for just ¥280 (and beer for ¥150). You won't regret 'splurging' on the ごまだれそば (*goma-dare soba;* buckwheat noodles with sesame dipping sauce) for ¥380. Look for the stone mill in the window and order from the vending machine. (嵯峨谷; 2-25-7 Dōgenzaka, Shibuya-ku; noodles from ¥280; ⏰24hr; ✐; ⎘JR Yamanote line to Shibuya, Hachikō exit)

Drinking

Good Beer Faucets
BAR

14 Map p72, B3

With 40 shiny taps, Good Beer Faucets has one of the city's best selections of Japanese craft brews and regularly draws a full house of locals and expats. The interior is chrome and concrete (and not at all grungy). Come for happy hour (5pm to 8pm Monday to Thursday, 4pm to 7pm Sunday) and get ¥200 off any beer. (グッドビアフォウセッツ; http://shibuya.goodbeerfaucets.jp; 2nd fl, 1-29-1 Shōtō, Shibuya-ku; beer from ¥800; ⏰5pm-midnight Mon-Thu & Sat, to 3am Fri, 4-11pm Sun; 🛜; 🚉JR Yamanote line to Shibuya, Hachikō exit)

Womb
CLUB

15 Map p72, B4

A long-time (in club years, at least) fixture on the Tokyo scene, Womb gets a lot of big-name international DJs playing mostly house and techno. Frenetic lasers and strobes splash across the heaving crowds, which usually jam all four floors. Warning: can get sweaty. (ウーム; ☎5459-0039; www.womb.co.jp; 2-16 Maruyama-chō, Shibuya-ku; cover ¥2000-4000; ⏰11pm-late Fri & Sat, 4-10pm Sun; 🚉JR Yamanote line to Shibuya, Hachikō exit)

Beat Cafe
BAR

16 Map p72, B4

Join an eclectic mix of local and international regulars at this comforta-bly shabby bar among the nightclubs and love hotels of Dōgenzaka. It's a known hang-out for musicians and music fans; check the website for info on parties (and after parties). Look for Gateway Studio on the corner; the bar is in the basement. (www.facebook.com/beatcafe; Basement fl, 2-13-5 Dōgenzaka, Shibuya-ku; drinks from ¥500; ⏰7pm-5am; 🚉JR Yamanote line to Shibuya, Hachikō exit)

Shidax Village
KARAOKE

17 Map p72, E2

Topped by a massive red neon sign, Shidax outshines all the other karaoke joints in the neighbourhood with spacious rooms and hundreds of English songs. A *nomihōdai* course (all you-can drink, two hours for ¥2040) is a sure bet for overcoming any lingering shyness. Nonsmoking

◯ Local Life
Nonbei-yokochō

Nonbei-yokochō is a narrow nightlife strip along the JR tracks, a collection of old wooden buildings that predates pretty much everything else in Shibuya. If you fancy a drink, check out teeny-tiny **Tight** (タイト; Map p72, E3; www.tight-tokyo.com; 2nd fl, 1-25-10 Shibuya, Shibuya-ku; drinks from ¥500; ⏰6pm-2am Mon-Sat, to midnight Sun; 🚉JR Yamanote line to Shibuya, Hachikō exit) – named for the tight fit around the bar. It has a big picture window in front.

rooms are available; rates are cheaper before 6pm. (シダックスビレッジ; 📞3461-9356; 1-12-13 Jinnan, Shibuya-ku; per 30min Mon-Thu ¥580, Fri-Sun ¥610; 🕙11am-5am Sun-Thu, to 6am Fri & Sat; 🚆JR Yamanote line to Shibuya, Hachikō exit)

Entertainment

WWW
LIVE MUSIC

 18   Map p72, D2

Tokyo's newest, big-hitting music venue used to be an art-house cinema. It still has the tiered floor (though the seats are gone) so everyone can see the stage. The line-up varies from indie pop to punk to electronica, but this is one of those rare venues where you could turn up just about any night and hear something good. (www-shibuya.jp/index.html; 13-17 Udagawa-chō, Shibuya-ku; tickets ¥2000-5000; 🚆JR Yamanote line to Shibuya, Hachikō exit)

Club Quattro
LIVE MUSIC

 19   Map p72, C3

This small, intimate venue has the feel of a slick nightclub. Though there's no explicit musical focus, emphasis is on rock and roll and world music, generally of high quality. Expect a more grown-up, artsy crowd than the club's location – near Center-gai – might lead you to expect. (クラブクアトロ; 📞3477-8750; www.club-quattro.com; 32-13-4 Udagawa-chō, Shibuya-ku; tickets ¥3000-4000; 🚆JR Yamanote line to Shibuya, Hachikō exit)

Shopping

Tōkyū Hands
VARIETY

 20 🔒 Map p72, C2

This DIY and *zakka* (miscellaneous goods) store has eight fascinating floors of everything you didn't know you needed. Like reflexology slippers, bee-venom face masks and cartoon-character-shaped rice-ball moulds. It's perfect for souvenir hunting too. (東急ハンズ; http://shibuya.tokyu-hands.co.jp; 12-18 Udagawa-chō, Shibuya-ku; 🕙10am-8.30pm; 🚆JR Yamanote line to Shibuya, Hachikō exit)

Fake Tokyo
FASHION

 21 🔒 Map p72, D3

This is one of the best places in the city to discover hot new Japanese designers. It's actually two shops in one: downstairs is Candy, full of brash, unisex streetwear; upstairs is Sister, which specialises in more ladylike items, both new and vintage. Look for the 'Fake Tokyo' banners out front. (📞5456-9892; www.faketokyo.com; 18-4 Udagawa-chō, Shibuya-ku; 🕙noon-10pm; 🚆JR Yamanote line to Shibuya, Hachikō exit)

Shibuya 109
FASHION

 22 🔒 Map p72, D3

See all those dolled-up teens walking around Shibuya? This is where they shop. Nicknamed *marukyū,* this cylindrical tower houses dozens of small boutiques, each with their own carefully styled look. Even if you don't

Shibuya Center-gai (p74)

intend to buy anything, you can't understand Shibuya without making a stop here. (渋谷109, Ichimarukyū; www.shibuya109.jp/en/top; 2-29-1 Dōgenzaka, Shibuya-ku; ☉10am-9pm; 🚃JR Yamanote line to Shibuya, Hachikō exit)

Parco   DEPARTMENT STORE

23 🔒 Map p72, D2

Not your typical fussy department store, Parco customers are more likely to be art-school students than ladies who lunch. Lots of Japanese fashion designers have shops here. (パルコ;

☎3464-5111; www.parco-shibuya.com; 15-1 Udagawa-chō, Shibuya-ku; ☉10am-9pm; 🚃JR Yamanote line to Shibuya, Hachikō exit)

Loft   VARIETY

24 🔒 Map p72, D3

This emporium of homewares, stationery and accessories specialises in all that is cute and covetable. The 1st floor is particularly ripe for souvenir-hunting. (ロフト; ☎3462-3807; www.loft.co.jp; 18-2 Udagawa-chō, Shibuya-ku; ☉10am-9pm; 🚃JR Yamanote line to Shibuya, Hachikō exit)

Local Life
Hanging Out in Shimo-Kitazawa

The narrow streets of 'Shimokita' are barely passable by cars, meaning a streetscape like a dollhouse version of Tokyo. It's been a favourite haunt for generations of students and there's a lively street scene all afternoon and evening, especially on weekends. If hippies – not bureaucrats – ran Tokyo, the city would look a lot more like Shimo-Kitazawa.

Getting There

🚋 The Keiō Inokashira line connects Shibuya with Shimo-Kitazawa; the Odakyū line connects Shinjuku with Shimo-Kitazawa.

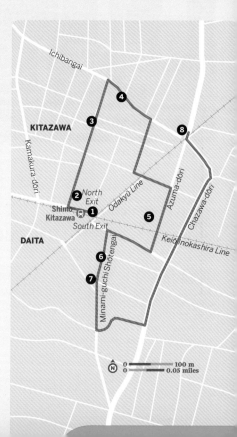

❶ An Old Market

Take the north exit from Shimo-Kitazawa Station and head right until you see the entrance to an old, post-WWII **covered market**. On its last legs (and scheduled to be demolished), it's a beloved symbol of the neighbourhood. A few vendors still stubbornly run shops here, and will until the end.

❷ DIY Fashion

Next stop: **Shimokita Garage Department** (東洋百貨店; 2-25-8 Kitazawa, Setagaya-ku; ⏱noon-8pm; 🚉Keiō Inokashira line to Shimo-Kitazawa, north exit), a not-quite-so-dilapidated covered market, with stalls selling DIY accessories and secondhand clothes. Colourful murals mark the entrance.

❸ Vintage Shopping

The bohemian vibe translates to a love of vintage clothing; **Haight & Ashbury** (2nd fl, 2-37-2 Kitazawa, Setagaya-ku; ⏱noon-10pm; 🚉Keiō Inokashira line to Shimo-Kitazawa, north exit) is the neighbourhood's best secondhand store.

❹ Espresso Break

Need a pick-me-up? **Bear Pond Espresso** (📞5454-2486; www.bear-pond.com; 2-36-12 Kitazawa, Setagaya-ku; coffee ¥300-700; ⏱10.30am-6pm Wed-Mon; 🚉Keiō Inokashira line to Shimo-Kitazawa, north exit) makes thick, syrupy espresso that has inspired a militant following. Espresso is only served until 1pm Thursday to Monday, but other coffee drinks are served all day.

❺ Fringe Theatres

Along Azuma-dōri – typical Shimokita with low-slung buildings and retro street signs – is Tokyo's underground theatre district. There are half-a-dozen theatres here in a span of a few blocks, including the **Honda Theatre** (本多劇場; www.honda-geki.com; 2-10-15 Kitazawa, Shibuya-ku; 🚉Keiō Inokashira line to Shimo-Kitazawa, south exit), and a complementary artsy vibe.

❻ The Southside

Compared to the more laid-back northside, Shimokita's southside is an entertainment centre, with bars and live-music houses. Bright, bustling **Minami-guchi Shōtengai** is the main drag.

❼ Izakaya Dinner

Duck down a side street and through the door curtains of **Shirube** (汁べゑ; 📞3413-3785; 2-18-2 Kitazawa, Setagaya-ku; dishes ¥580-880; ⏱5.30pm-midnight; 📝; 🚉Keiō Inokashira line to Shimo-Kitazawa, south exit), a rowdy, popular *izakaya* (Japanese pub-eatery) that mixes classic dishes with fusion ones. Book on weekends and don't miss the *aburi-saba* (blowtorch-grilled mackerel).

❽ Never Never Land

Twinkling lights mark the late-night haunt **Never Never Land** (ネヴァーネヴァーランド; 3-19-3 Kitazawa, Setagaya-ku; ⏱6pm-2am; 🚉Keiō Inokashira line to Shimo-Kitazawa, north exit), a classic Shimokita bar: smokey, loud and filled with bohemian characters.

Explore

Harajuku & Aoyama

Harajuku is one of Tokyo's biggest draws, both for its stately shrine, Meiji-jingū, and its colourful street fashion. The boutique-lined boulevard Omote-sandō is a must-see for fans of contemporary architecture. Harajuku also has several excellent art museums, and you can spend a rewarding day bouncing between the traditional and the modern while indulging in excellent restaurants, cafes and boutiques.

The Sights in a Day

🔅 Get an early start and beat the crowds to **Meiji-jingū** (p84), Tokyo's most famous Shintō shrine. If you're visiting on a weekend in the warmer months, check out the scene at **Yoyogi-kōen** (p88). Otherwise, make a beeline for the teenage-fashion parade down **Takeshita-dōri** (p88). Make a worthwhile detour to the **Ukiyo-e Ōta Memorial Art Museum** (p88), before breaking for lunch at local favourite **Harajuku Gyōza-rō** (p91).

🔆 Spend the afternoon making your way down the boutique-lined boulevard **Omote-sandō** (p88), gawking at the impressive architecture. Duck into the alleyways of Ura-Hara, to see some off-the-wall fashions and to take a peak into the equally off-the-wall **Design Festa** (p90). Grab a coffee at one of the neighbourhood's many cafes, such as **Omotesando Koffee** (p92). Leave yourself an hour to explore the galleries of the **Nezu Museum** (p88) at the far end of Omote-sandō, in Aoyama.

🌙 Watch the sunset over a glass of wine at **Two Rooms** (p92), then treat yourself to a deluxe seafood spread at **Yanmo** (p90) or tender *tonkatsu* (deep-fried pork cutlet) at **Maisen** (p91).

👁 **Top Sights**

Meiji-jingū (p84)

 Best of Tokyo

Parks & Gardens
Yoyogi-kōen (p88)

Galleries & Museums
Ukiyo-e Ōta Memorial Art Museum (p88)

Nezu Museum (p88)

Eating
Yanmo (p90)

Shopping & Markets
Laforet (p94)

Sou-Sou (p94)

Pop Culture
KiddyLand (p94)

Takeshita-dōri (p88)

Getting There

🚃 **Train** The JR Yamanote line stops at Harajuku; the JR Sōbu line stops at Sendagaya.

Ⓢ **Subway** The Chiyoda and Fukutoshin lines stop at Meiji-jingū-mae, near JR Harajuku Station. The Chiyoda, Ginza and Hanzōmon lines stop at Omote-sandō; the Ginza line continues to Gaienmae.

Top Sights
Meiji-jingū

Tokyo's grandest Shintō shrine is dedicated to the Emperor Meiji and Empress Shōken. Emperor Meiji's reign (1867–1912) coincided with the country's transformation from an isolationist, feudal state to a modern nation. Constructed in 1920, the shrine was destroyed in WWII air raids and rebuilt in 1958; however, unlike many of Japan's postwar reconstructions, Meiji-jingū has an authentic feel. The shrine occupies only a small fraction of the sprawling forested grounds, which contain 120,000 trees collected from around Japan.

明治神宮

◉ Map p86, A2

www.meijijingu.or.jp

1-1 Yoyogi Kamizono-chō, Shibuya-ku

⏱ dawn-dusk

🚇 JR Yamanote line to Harajuku, Omote-sandō exit

Meiji-jingū

Don't Miss

The Gates

Towering *torii* (gates) mark the entrance to the shrine and sacred space. The largest gate, created from a 1500-year-old Taiwanese cypress, stands 12m high. Along the path you'll also see rows of decorative sake barrels – gifts to the shrine (and a favourite of photographers).

The Font

Approaching the main shrine, the *temizuya* (font) is on the left. Shintō places a premium on purity, so visitors perform a cleansing ritual. Use the dipper to pour water over your left hand, then your right (without letting the water drip back into the pool). Fill your left hand with water and rinse out your mouth. Rinse your left hand a final time.

The Main Shrine

The main shrine is made of cypress from the Kiso region of Nagano. To make the customary offering, toss a coin – ¥5 coins are considered the luckiest – into the box, bow twice, clap your hands twice, say a prayer if you like and bow again. Clapping is said to attract the gods' attention.

Meiji-jingū-gyoen

Meiji-jingū-gyoen (明治神宮御苑; Inner Garden; admission ¥500; ☉9am-4.30pm, to 4pm Nov-Feb; 🚃JR Yamanote line to Harajuku, Omote-Sandō exit) is a landscaped garden on the grounds of the shrine that once belonged to a feudal estate. When the grounds passed into imperial hands, the emperor himself designed the iris garden to please the empress. The entrance is on the right, about half-way down the path to the main shrine.

☑ Top Tips

▶ Every day at 8am and 2pm a priest strikes a large drum as part of a ritual offering of food to the deities enshrined here. This is the best time to visit.

▶ Admission is free.

▶ If you're lucky, you may also catch a traditional wedding procession – just try not to get in the way.

▶ You'll likely attract guards if you get your camera out too close to the main shrine. The rule of photo-taking here is this: if there's a roof over your head, it's a no-go.

✗ Take a Break

At the entrance to the shrine, overlooking the wooded path, **Mori no Terrace** (杜のテラス; Map p86, A5; 1-1 Yoyogi Kamizono-chō, Shibuya-ku; coffee ¥280; ☉9am-4.30pm) serves coffee, pastries and ice cream.

Purveyor of delicious dumplings, Harajuku Gyōza-rō (p91) is a 10-minute walk away.

Shuto Expwy No 4

Jingū-gaien

National Stadium

Meiji-kōen

Galen-nishi-dōri

Watari Museum of Contemporary Art

6

Shinjuku-gyoen (Shinjuku Park)

Tokyo Metropolitan Gymnasium

SENDAGAYA

18

SHIBUYA-KU

21　11

Moshi Moshi Information Space

Design Festa

7

Meiji-dōri

Meiji-dōri

Kita-sandō

Togō-jinja

15

Takeshita-dōri

1

Takeshita-dōri

Harajuku

Kita-sandō

Meiji-jingū Kaikan

Minami-sandō

Meiji-jingū

Meiji-jingū Gyoen

Sights

Takeshita-dōri
STREET

1 Map p86, B4

This is Tokyo's famous teen-fashion bazaar, where trendy duds sit alongside the trappings of various fashion subcultures (colourful tutus for the *decora;* Victorian dresses for the gothic Lolitas). Be warned: this pedestrian alley is a pilgrimage site for teens from all over Japan, which means it can get packed. (竹下通り; JR Yamanote line to Harajuku, Takeshita exit)

Ukiyo-e Ōta Memorial Museum of Art
MUSEUM

2 Map p86, B5

This small, peaceful museum houses the excellent *ukiyo-e* (woodblock prints) collection of Ōta Seizo, the former head of the Toho Life Insurance Company. Seasonal, thematic exhibitions are easily digested in an hour and usually include a few works by masters such as Hokusai and Hiroshige. (浮世絵太田記念美術館; 3403-0880; www.ukiyoe-ota-muse.jp; 1-10-10 Jingūmae, Shibuya-ku; adult ¥700-1000, child free; 10.30am-5.30pm Tue-Sun, closed 27th to end of month; JR Yamanote line to Harajuku, Omote-sandō exit)

Nezu Museum
MUSEUM

3 Map p86, E7

Nezu Museum offers a striking blend of old and new: a renowned collection of Japanese, Chinese and Korean antiquities in a gallery space designed by contemporary architect Kuma Kengo. Select items from the extensive collection are displayed in seasonal exhibitions. (根津美術館; 3400-2536; www.nezu-muse.or.jp; 6-5-1 Minami-Aoyama, Minato-ku; adult/student/child ¥1000/800/free, special exhibitions ¥200 extra; 10am-5pm Tue-Sun, S Ginza line to Omote-sandō, exit A5)

Take a Break **Nezu Café** (coffee ¥650; 10am-5pm) is an attractive glass box in the garden behind the museum.

Omote-sandō
STREET

4 Map p86, D6

This regal boulevard was originally designed as the official approach to Meiji-jingū. Now it's a fashionable strip lined with high-end boutiques. Those designer shops come in designer buildings, which means Omote-sandō is also one of the best places in the city to see contemporary architecture. (表参道; S Ginza line to Omote-sandō, exits A3 & B4, JR Yamanote line to Harajuku, Omote-sandō exit)

Yoyogi-kōen
PARK

5 Map p86, A5

If it's a sunny and warm weekend afternoon, you can count on there being a crowd lazing around the large grassy expanse that is Yoyogi-kōen. You can also usually find revellers and noise-makers of all stripes, from hula-hoopers to African drum circles to a group of retro greasers dancing

Understand
Religion Today

Visit Omote-sandō – originally designed as the official approach to Meiji-jingū – on a weekend and you'll see Tokyoites lining the pavements, waiting for a seat at the latest hot restaurant. Meanwhile, Meiji-jingū is full of tourists. Yet over the first three days of the New Year, about three million people visit the shrine to ring in the New Year in the traditional way. While religion may play little part in the daily lives of most Tokyoites, when tradition calls they turn out in a big way.

Annual Observances

Ganjitsu (New Year's Day) is the most auspicious day of the Japanese calendar. At midnight on 1 January, crowds convene at temples, where bells are rung 108 times to cast off the worldly desires of the previous year, and at shrines, where people pray for health, happiness and prosperity. In Tokyo, Meiji-jingū is the most popular shrine to visit and Sensō-ji (p134) is the most popular temple.

Another important annual event is **O-Bon**: three days in mid-August to honour the dead, when their spirits are said to return to the earth. Many Tokyoites return to their home towns to sweep the graves of their ancestors and to participate in *bon-odori* (folk dances).

Rites of Passage

Rites of passage are marked, as for centuries, with a visit to a shrine or temple. Japan's two religious institutions – its native Shintō, an animist belief system that sees godliness in trees, rocks and animals, and Buddhism, which arrived via China in the 7th century – have long coexisted.

Generally, Shintō concerns itself with this life: births and marriage, for example, are celebrated at shrines. If you're lucky, you might catch such a ceremony, where celebrants wear elaborate kimonos. Meanwhile, Buddhism deals with the afterlife: funerals and memorial rites take place at temples.

around a boom box. It's an excellent place for a picnic and probably the only place in the city where you can reasonably toss a frisbee without fear of hitting someone. (代々木公園; R JR Yamanote line to Harajuku, Omote-sandō exit)

Watari Museum of Contemporary Art

MUSEUM

6 ◉ Map p86, D4

This progressive and often provocative museum was built in 1990 to a design by Swiss architect Mario Botta. Exhibits range from retrospectives of established art-world figures (such as Yayoi Kusama and Nam June Paik) to graffiti and landscape artists – with some exhibitions spilling onto the surrounding streets. (ワタリウム美術館, Watari-Um; ☑3402-3001; www.watarium.co.jp; 3-7-6 Jingūmae, Shibuya-ku; adult/student ¥1000/800; ⊙11am-7pm Tue & Thu-Sun, to 9pm Wed; S Ginza line to Gaienmae, exit 3)

Design Festa

GALLERY

7 ◉ Map p86, C4

Design Festa has been a leader in Tokyo's DIY art scene for over a decade. The madhouse building itself is worth a visit; it's always evolving. Inside there are a dozen small galleries rented by the day. Design Festa also sponsors a twice-yearly exhibition, actually Asia's largest art fair, at Tokyo Big Sight. (デザインフェスタ; ☑3479-1442; www.designfestagallery.com; 3-20-2 Jingūmae, Shibuya-ku; admission free; ⊙11am-7pm; R JR Yamanote line to Harajuku, Takeshita exit)

Take a Break Funky *okonomiyaki* (savoury pancake) restaurant Sakura-tei is just out back.

Eating

Yanmo

SEAFOOD $$$

8 🍴 Map p86, D7

Fresh caught seafood from the nearby Izu Peninsula is the speciality at this upscale, yet unpretentious restaurant.

Understand
Harajuku Style

Harajuku is the city's living catwalk. It's also that rare place in Japan where unconventionality is rewarded: a country girl can get off a train, get a job at a local boutique and – with enough moxie and sartorial innovation – find herself on the pages of a national magazine within a year. Clerks and hair stylists set the trends in Harajuku, not the fashion glossies, as photographers from street-fashion magazines and websites stalk the neighbourhood looking for the next big thing. Every time someone declares Harajuku dead, another trend is born, inspiring a whole nation of teens.

If you're looking to splash out on a seafood dinner, this is a great place to do so. The reasonably priced courses include sashimi, and steamed and grilled fish. Lunch is a bargain, but you might have to queue. Reservations are essential for dinner. (やんも; www.yanmo.co.jp/aoyama/index.html; Basement, T Place Bldg, 5-5-25 Minami-Aoyama, Minato-ku; lunch/dinner course from ¥1100/7560; ⏰11.30am-2pm & 6-10.30pm Mon-Sat; Ⓢ Ginza line to Omote-sandō, exit A5)

Harajuku Gyōza-rō GYOZA $

9 Map p86, B5

Gyōza (dumplings) are the only thing on the menu here, but you won't hear any complaints from the regulars who queue up to get their fix. Have them *sui* (boiled) or *yaki* (pan-fried), with or without *niniku* (garlic) or *nira* (chives) – they're all delicious. Expect to wait on weekends. (原宿餃子楼; 6-4-2 Jingūmae, Shibuya-ku; 6 gyōza ¥290; ⏰11.30am-4.30am; Ⓡ JR Yamanote line to Harajuku, Omote-sandō exit)

Maisen TONKATSU $

10 Map p86, D5

You could order something else (like fried shrimp), but everyone else will be ordering the famous *tonkatsu*. There are different grades of pork on the menu, including prized *kurobuta* (black pig), but even the cheapest is melt-in-your-mouth divine. The restaurant is housed in an old public bathhouse. A takeaway window serves delicious *tonkatsu sando* (sandwich). (まい泉;

http://mai-sen.com; 4-8-5 Jingūmae, Shibuya-ku; lunch/dinner from ¥995/1680; ⏰11am-10pm; Ⓢ Ginza line to Omote-sandō, exit A2)

Mominoki House ORGANIC $$

11 Map p86, C4

Boho Tokyoites have been coming here for tasty macrobiotic fare since 1976. The casual, cosy dining room has seen some famous visitors too, such as Paul McCartney. Chef Yamada's menu is heavily vegetarian, but also includes free-range chicken and *Ezo shika* (Hokkaidō venison, ¥4800). (もみの木ハウス; http://omotesando.mominokihouse.net; 2-18-5 Jingūmae, Shibuya-ku; lunch/dinner sets from ¥800/3200; ⏰11.30am-10pm; ✒; Ⓡ JR Yamanote line to Harajuku, Takeshita exit)

Sakura-tei OKONOMIYAKI $

Grill your own *okonomiyaki* (savoury pancakes) at this funky place inside the gallery Design Festa (see 7 ◉ Map p86, C4). During lunch (11am to 3pm) you can get 90 minutes of all you can eat, plus a drink, for just ¥1060. (さくら亭; ☎3479-0039; www.sakuratei.co.jp; 3-20-1 Jingūmae, Shibuya-ku; okonomiyaki ¥950-1350; ⏰11am-11pm; 📷; 🚇JR Yamanote line to Harajuku, Takeshita exit)

Pariya
INTERNATIONAL $

12 🍴 Map p86, C7

Pariya is the local cafeteria for the fashionable set. Grab a tray and choose one main, one salad and one side dish (or two salads and a side for veggies). Typical dishes include shrimp croquettes and curried potato salad. There are colourful cupcakes and gelato for dessert. (パリヤ; 3-12-14 Kita-Aoyama, Minato-ku; meals from ¥1030; ⏰11.30am-11pm; 📷; 🚇Ginza line to Omote-sandō, exit B2)

Drinking

Two Rooms
BAR

13 🍷 Map p86, D7

Expect a crowd dressed like they don't care that wine by the glass starts at ¥1500. You can eat here too, but the real scene is at night by the bar. Call ahead (staff speak English) on Friday or Saturday night to reserve a table on the terrace, which has sweeping views towards the Shinjuku skyline. (トゥールームス; ☎3498-0002; www.tworooms.jp; 5th fl, AO Bldg, 3-11-7 Kita-Aoyama, Minato-ku; ⏰11.30am-2am Mon-Sat, to 10pm Sun; 🚇Ginza line to Omote-sandō, exit B2)

Omotesando Koffee
CAFE

14 🍷 Map p86, D5

Tokyo's most *oshare* (stylish) coffee stand is a minimalist cube set up inside a half-century-old traditional house. Be prepared to circle the block trying to find it, but know that an immaculate macchiato and a seat in the garden await you. (http://ooo-koffee.com; 4-15-3 Jingūmae, Shibuya-ku; espresso ¥250; ⏰10am-7pm; 🚇Ginza line to Omote-sandō, exit A2)

Harajuku Taproom
PUB

15 🍷 Map p86, B4

Baird's Brewery is one of Japan's most successful and consistently good craft breweries. This is one of its two Tokyo outposts, where you can sample more than a dozen of its beers on tap; try the top-selling Rising Sun Pale Ale. Japanese pub-style food is served as well. (原宿タップルーム; http://bairdbeer.com/en/taproom; 2nd fl, 1-20-13 Jingūmae, Shibuya-ku; ⏰5pm-midnight Mon-Fri, noon-midnight Sat & Sun; 🚇JR Yamanote line to Harajuku, Takeshita exit)

Montoak
CAFE

16 🍷 Map p86, B5

This smoky glass cube is a calm, dimly lit retreat from the busy streets. It's perfect for holing up with a pot of tea or carafe of wine and watching the crowds go by. Or, if the weather is nice, score a seat on the terrace. (モントーク; 6-1-9 Jingūmae, Shibuya-ku; ⏰11am-3am; 🚇JR Yamanote line to Harajuku, Omote-sandō exit)

Dancers practicing at Yoyogi-kōen (p88)

Entertainment

Jingū Baseball Stadium
BASEBALL

 17 ⭐ Map p86, E3

Jingū Baseball Stadium, built in 1926, is home to the Yakult Swallows, Tokyo's number-two team (but number one when it comes to fan loyalty). Pick up tickets from the booth in front of the stadium; same-day outfield tickets cost just ¥1600 (¥500 for children) and are usually available. Night games start at 6pm; weekend games start around 2pm. (神宮球場; Jingū Kyūjō; ☎3404-8999; www.jingu-stadium.com; 3-1 Kasumigaoka-machi, Shinjuku-ku; tickets ¥1600-4600; Ⓢ Ginza line to Gaienmae, exit 3)

National Nō Theatre
THEATRE

18 ⭐ Map p86, C1

The traditional music, poetry and dances that *nō* (stylised Japanese dance-drama) is famous for unfold here on an elegant cypress stage. Each seat has a small screen that can display an English translation of the dialogue. Shows take place only a few times a month. (国立能楽堂; Kokuritsu Nō-gakudō; ☎3423-1331; www.ntj.jac.go.jp/english; 4-18-1 Sendagaya, Shibuya-ku; tickets from ¥2600; Ⓡ JR Sōbu line to Sendagaya)

Shopping

Laforet

FASHION

19 🔒 Map p86, B5

Laforet has been a beacon of cutting-edge Harajuku style for decades. Don't let the Topshop on the ground floor fool you; lots of quirky, cult favourite brands still cut their teeth here. (ラフォーレ; www.laforet.ne.jp; 1-11-6 Jingūmae, Shibuya-ku; ⏱11am-8pm; 🚉JR Yamanote line to Harajuku, Omote-sandō exit)

Local Life

Ura-Hara

Ura-Hara (literally 'behind Harajuku') is the nickname for the maze of backstreets behind Omote-sandō. You'll find the eccentric shops and secondhand stores from which Harajuku hipsters cobble together their head-turning looks. Two good places to start are **Dog** (ドッグ; Map p86, C4; www.dog-hjk.com/index.html; Basement, 3-23-3 Jingūmae, Shibuya-ku; ⏱noon-8pm; 🚉JR Yamanote line to Harajuku, Takeshita exit), which stocks bold and brash vintage and remake items loved by club kids and stylists, and **6% Doki Doki** (ロクパーセントドキドキ; Map p86, C5; www.dokidoki6.com; 2nd fl, 4-28-16 Jingūmae, Shibuya-ku; ⏱noon-8pm; 🚉JR Yamanote line to Harajuku, Omote-sandō exit), which specialises in candy-coloured accessories.

Sou-Sou

FASHION

20 🔒 Map p86, E8

Sou-Sou gives traditional Japanese clothing items – such as split-toed *tabi* socks and *haori* (coats with kimono-like sleeves) – a contemporary spin. It is best known for producing the steel-toed, rubber-soled *tabi* shoes worn by Japanese construction workers in fun, playful designs. (そうそう; 📞3407-7877; http://sousounetshop.jp; 5-3-10 Minami-Aoyama, Minato-ku; ⏱11am-8pm; 🚇Ginza line to Omote-sandō, exit A5)

Musubi

SPECIALTY SHOP

21 🔒 Map p86, C4

Furoshiki are versatile squares of cloth that can be folded and knotted to make shopping bags and gift wrap. This shop sells pretty ones in both traditional and contemporary patterns. There is usually an English-speaking clerk who can show you how to tie them, or you can pick up one of the English-language books sold here. (むす美; http://kyoto-musubi.com; 2-31-8 Jingūmae, Shibuya-ku; ⏱11am-7pm Thu-Tue; 🚉JR Yamanote line to Harajuku, Takeshita exit)

KiddyLand

TOYS

22 🔒 Map p86, B5

This multistorey toy emporium is packed to the rafters with character goods. It's not just for kids either; you'll spot plenty of adults on a nostalgia trip down the Hello Kitty aisle. (キデイランド; www.kiddyland.co.jp/en/index.html; 6-1-9 Jingūmae, Shibuya-ku; ⏱10am-9pm; 🚉JR Yamanote line to Harajuku, Omote-sandō exit)

Bedrock FASHION

23 Map p86, C5

Walking into Bedrock is like stepping into Keith Richards' boudoir, or the costume closet for Pirates of the Caribbean. Enter through a secret staircase in the back of the Forbidden Fruit juice bar. (ベッドロック; 4-12-10 Jingūmae, Shibuya-ku; 🕙11am-9pm, to 8pm Sun; 🅂Ginza line to Omote-sandō, exit A2)

Comme des Garçons FASHION

24 Map p86, D7

Designer Kawakubo Rei threw a wrench in the fashion machine in the early '80s with her dark, asymmetrical designs. That her work doesn't appear as shocking today as it once did speaks volumes for her far-reaching success. This eccentric, vaguely disorienting architectural creation is her brand's flagship store. (コム・デ・ギャルソン; www.comme-des-garcons.com; 5-2-1 Minami-Aoyama, Minato-ku; 🕙11am-8pm; 🅂Ginza line to Omote-sandō, exit A5)

Gallery Kawano KIMONO

25 Map p86, D6

Gallery Kawano has a good selection of vintage kimonos in decent shape, priced reasonably (about ¥5000 to ¥15,000). The staff will help you try one on and pick out a matching *obi* (sash); they're less excited about customers who try things on but don't intend to buy. (ギャラリー川野; www.gallery-kawano.com; 4-4-9 Jingūmae, Shibuya-ku; 🕙11am-6pm; 🚉Ginza line to Omote-sandō, exit A2)

Tokyo's Tokyo SOUVENIRS

26 Map p86, B5

Tokyo's Tokyo is betting that you'd love to find something slightly wacky, pop-culture inflected and 'only in Tokyo' to bring home with you. It's stocked with accessories from local fashion designers, surprisingly useful gadgets and other fun trinkets. (トーキョーズトーキョー; 5th fl, Tōkyū Plaza, 4-30-3 Jingūmae, Shibuya-ku; 🕙11am-9pm; 🚉JR Yamanote line to Harajuku, Omote-sandō exit)

Oriental Bazaar SOUVENIRS

27 Map p86, C6

Oriental Bazaar stocks a wide selection of souvenirs at very reasonable prices. Items to be found here include fans, pottery, *yukata* (light summer kimonos) and T-shirts, some made in Japan, but others not (read the labels). (オリエンタルバザー; www.oriental-bazaar.co.jp; 5-9-13 Jingūmae, Shibuya-ku; 🕙10am-6pm Mon-Wed & Fri, to 7pm Sat & Sun; 🚉JR Yamanote line to Harajuku, Omote-sandō exit)

Condomania SPECIALITY SHOP

28 Map p86, B5

This irreverent outpost must be Tokyo's cheekiest rendezvous point. Popular items include *omamori* (traditional good-luck charms) with condoms tucked inside. (コンドマニア; 6-30-1 Jingūmae, Shibuya-ku; 🕙11am-9.30pm; 🚉JR Yamanote line to Harajuku, Omote-sandō exit)

Explore

Shinjuku

Here in Shinjuku, much of what makes Tokyo tick is crammed into one busy district: upscale department stores, anachronistic shanty bars, buttoned-up government offices, swarming crowds, streetside video screens, leafy parks, racy nightlife, hidden shrines and soaring skyscrapers. It's a fantastic introduction to Tokyo today, with all its highs and lows.

The Sights in a Day

☀ The morning – usually the clearest time of day – is the best time to visit the **Tokyo Metropolitan Government Offices** (p101), for views over the city from the 45th-floor observatory (otherwise come back for the night view). Back on the ground, wind your way through the skyscraper district of Nishi-Shinjuku, checking out the art at **Shinjuku I-Land** (p101). Then head over to department store **Isetan** (p107) and pick up a *bentō* (boxed meal) from the *depachika* (department store basement food hall) for lunch.

☀ Walk to **Shinjuku-gyoen** (p101) for a picnic on the lawn and spend a relaxing hour strolling through the park. Then return to the hustle and bustle for a bit of shopping – in Shinjuku you can get just about anything, including fashion, electronics and music.

☾ Shinjuku is famous for its nightlife. Start with skewers of *yakitori* (grilled chicken) in atmospheric **Omoide-yokochō** (p102). Then catch a jazz show at **Shinjuku Pit Inn** (p107) or a cabaret spectacle at **Robot Restaurant** (p106). For a nightcap, visit **Zoetrope** (p104) – Japan's best whisky bar.

For a local's night out in Shinjuku, see p98.

🔍 **Local Life**

East Shinjuku at Night (p98)

 **Best of Tokyo**

Architecture
Tokyo Metropolitan Government Offices (p101)

Parks & Gardens
Shinjuku-gyoen (p101)

Food
Nagi (p99)

Shopping & Markets
Isetan (p107)

Nightlife & Live Music
Zoetrope (p104)
Golden Gai (p99)

Gay & Lesbian
Advocates Café (p105)

Getting There

🚃 **Train** The JR Yamanote and Chūō-Sōbu lines stop at Shinjuku Station.

Ⓢ **Subway** The Marunouchi, Shinjuku and Ōedo lines run through Shinjuku. The Marunouchi, Fukutoshin and Shinjuku lines stop at Shinjuku-sanchōme, convenient for east Shinjuku. The Ōedo line stops at Tochōmae.

Local Life
East Shinjuku at Night

East Shinjuku is Tokyo's largest – and liveliest – nightlife district. The size and depth means there is truly something for everyone, from flashy cabarets to bohemian hole-in-the walls, neon-lit karaoke parlours to bars for every fetish under the sun. Come dark, a motley cast of characters hits the town to shed the day's anxieties and to let loose.

❶ Take the East Exit
On a Friday or Saturday night, the world's busiest train station is particularly busy – and just about everyone is heading to the east exit for Shinjuku's infamous nightlife. From the east exit, follow the station signs for Kabukichō. When you emerge, you should see the glowing screen of Studio Alta, Shinjuku's de facto meeting spot.

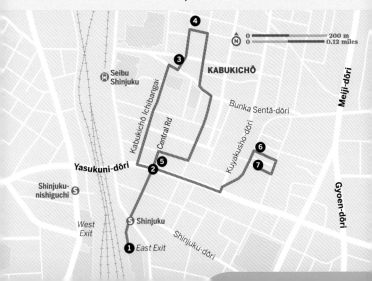

2 Bask in the Lights of Yasukuni-dōri

This is east Shinjuku's main drag, where *izakaya* (Japanese pub-eateries) are stacked several stories high, along with karaoke joints, all-night noodle shops, convenience stores and acres of neon. Touts for bars and restaurants stalk the pavements, waving menus and handing out coupons, the cries of: *Izakaya ikaga desu ka*? ('How about an izakaya?') rising above the din.

3 Tiptoe through Kabukichō

North of Yasukuni-dōri is the neighbourhood of Kabukichō, Tokyo's most notorious red-light district. The entrance is marked by a red electric *torii* (gate). Here, it's wall-to-wall hostess (and host!) clubs (bars where pretty people are employed to heap compliments and expensive drinks on customers) cabarets and love hotels. It's generally safe to walk through, though we don't recommend going alone (or going inside anywhere).

4 Take a Swing at Oslo Batting Center

An odd oasis of wholesome fun, **Oslo Batting Center** (オスローバッティングセンター; www.oslo.ecweb.jp; 2nd fl, Oslo Bldg, 2-34-5 Kabukichō, Shinjuku-ku; ⊙10am-1am; ⊠JR Yamanote line to Shinjuku, east exit) offers another way to blow off steam in Kabukichō. It's ¥300 for 20 pitches if you feel like taking a swing. There's an arcade on the ground floor.

5 Rummage through Don Quijote

Back on Yasukuni-dōri, you can't miss the fluorescent-lit bargain castle that is **Don Quijote** (ドン・キホーテ; ☑5291-9211; www.donki.com; 1-16-5 Kabukichō, Shinjuku-ku; ⊙24hr; ⊠JR Yamanote line to Shinjuku, east exit). It's filled to the brim with weird loot. Though it's now a national chain, it started as a rare (at the time) 24-hour store for the city's night workers.

6 Raise a Glass in Golden Gai

This is Tokyo's most ambient cluster of watering halls, a colony of narrow two-storey wooden buildings that was a black market in the post-WWII years. Each closet-sized bar is as unique and eccentric as the 'master' or 'mama' who runs it. While some may give tourists the cold shoulder, **Albatross G** (アルバトロスG; www.alba-s.com/index.html; 1-1-7 Kabukichō, Shinjuku-ku; cover charge ¥500, drinks from ¥500; ⊙7pm-5am; ⊠JR Yamanote line to Shinjuku, east exit) is a friendly place with a groovy interior.

7 Go for Late-Night Rāmen

A late-night bowl of *rāmen* (soup and noodles with a sprinkling of meat and vegetables) is a beloved Tokyo tradition. **Nagi** (凪; www.n-nagi.com; 2nd fl, Golden Gai G2, 1-1-10 Kabukichō, Shinjuku-ku; rāmen from ¥820; ⊙24hr; ⊠JR Yamanote line to Shinjuku, east exit), in Golden Gai, serves highly addictive noodles in a dark broth deeply flavoured with *niboshi* (dried sardines). Look for the red sign and the treacherous flight of stairs.

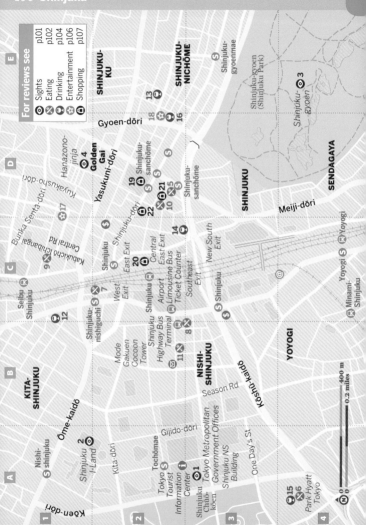

SHINJUKU-KU

SHINJUKU-NICHŌME

Gyoen-dōri

Hanazono-jinja

❹ 4 Golden Gai

Kuyakusho-dōri

Yasukuni-dōri

Shinjuku-sanchōme

Shinjuku-dōri

Shinjuku East Exit

Central East Exit

Bunka Senta-dōri

Kabukicho ichibangai Central Rd

Shinjuku West Exit

Seibu Shinjuku

Shinjuku-nishiguchi

Mode Gakuen Cocoon Tower

Shinjuku Highway Bus Terminal

Airport Limousine Bus Ticket Counter

Southeast Exit

New South Exit

Shinjuku

Meiji-dōri

SHINJUKU

SENDAGAYA

Shinjuku-gyoen (Shinjuku Park)

Shinjuku-gyoenmae

◉ 3 Shinjuku-gyoen

YOYOGI

Yoyogi

Minami-Shinjuku

KITA-SHINJUKU

Ōme-kaidō

Nishi-shinjuku

◉ 2 Shinjuku I-Land

Kita-dōri

Tokyo Tourist Information Center

Tochōmae

Tokyo Metropolitan Government Offices

◉ 1 Shinjuku Chūō-kōen

Gijidō-dōri

Shinjuku NS Building

Season Rd

One Day's St

Kōshū-kaidō

❹ 15 ❸ 6 Park Hyatt Tokyo

Kōen-dōri

400 m
0.2 miles

Sights

Tokyo Metropolitan Government Offices
BUILDING

 1 Map p100, A3

Tokyo's seat of power, designed by Tange Kenzō, looms large and looks somewhat like a pixelated cathedral. Take an elevator from the ground floor of Building 1 to one of the twin 202m-high observatories for panoramic views over the never-ending cityscape (the views are virtually the same from either tower). On a clear day, look west for a glimpse of Mt Fuji. (東京都庁; Tokyo Tochō; www.metro.tokyo.jp/ENGLISH/TMG/observat.htm; 2-8-1 Nishi-Shinjuku, Shinjuku-ku; admission free; ☉observatories 9.30am-11pm; ⑤Ōedo line to Tochōmae, exit A4)

Shinjuku I-Land
PUBLIC ART

2 Map p100, A1

An otherwise ordinary office complex, Shinjuku I-Land (1995) is home to more than a dozen public artworks, including one of Robert Indiana's *Love* sculptures and two *Tokyo Brushstroke* sculptures by Roy Liechtenstein. The courtyard, with stonework by Giulio Paolini and a dozen restaurants, makes for an attractive lunch or coffee stop. (新宿アイランド; 6-5-1 Nishi-Shinjuku, Shinjuku-ku; ⑤Marunouchi line to Nishi-Shinjuku)

Shinjuku-gyoen
PARK

3 Map p100, E4

Though Shinjuku-gyoen was designed as an imperial retreat (completed 1906), it's now definitively a park for everyone. The wide lawns make it a favourite for urbanites in need of a quick escape from the hurly-burly of city life. Don't miss the recently renovated greenhouse, with its giant lily pads and perfectly formed orchids, and the cherry blossoms in spring. (新宿御苑; ☎3350-0151; www.env.go.jp/garden/shinjukugyoen; 11 Naito-chō, Shinjuku-ku; adult/child ¥200/50; ☉9am-4.30pm Tue-Sun; ⑤Marunouchi line to Shinjuku-gyoenmae, exit 1)

Hanazono-jinja
SHINTO SHRINE

4 Map p100, D1

During the day merchants from nearby Kabukichō come to this Shintō shrine to pray for the solvency of their business ventures. At night, despite signs asking revellers to refrain, drinking and merrymaking carries over from the nearby bars onto the stairs here. (花園神社; 5-17 Shinjuku, Shinjuku-ku; ☉24hr; ⑤Marunouchi line to Shinjuku-sanchōme, exits B10 & E2)

 Top Tip

Navigating Shinjuku Station

Shinjuku Station is the world's busiest – three million people pass through daily. It's so big that the wrong exit can take you kilometres from where you want to be. Check the exit signs on the train platform and use the correct stairs – this will save you a lot of trouble above ground.

Eating

Nakajima

KAISEKI $

5 Map p100, D2

In the evening this Michelin-starred restaurant serves exquisite *kaiseki* (Japanese haute cuisine) dinners. On weekdays it also serves a set lunch of humble *iwashi* (sardines) for one-tenth the price; in the hands of Nakajima's chefs they're divine. The line for lunch starts to form shortly before the restaurant opens at 11.30am. Look for the white sign at the top of the stairs. (中嶋; ☏3356-4534; www. shinjyuku-nakajima.com; Basement, 3-32-5 Shinjuku, Shinjuku-ku; lunch/dinner from ¥800/8640; ⏰11.30am-2pm & 5.30-10pm Mon-Sat; ⓢMarunouchi line to Shinjuku-sanchōme, exit A1)

☑ Top Tip

Food Courts

Department stores usually have food courts on their top floors, as do the ones in Shinjuku Station. **Lumine** (ルミネ; Map p100, C3; www. lumine.ne.jp/shinjuku; Shinjuku Station, Shinjuku-ku; ⏰11am-11pm; ⓡJR Yamanote line to Shinjuku, south exit) and **Mylord** (ミロード; Map p100, C3; www.shinjuku-mylord.com; Shinjuku Station, Shinjuku-ku; ⏰11am-11pm; ⓡJR Yamanote line to Shinjuku, south exit) have the most reasonably priced options. It's an easy way to grab a meal without having to brave the crowds on the streets.

Kozue

JAPANESE $$$

6 Map p100, A4

It's hard to beat Kozue's combination of exquisite, seasonal Japanese cuisine, artisan crockery and soaring views over Shinjuku from the floor-to-ceiling windows. Reservations are essential. (梢; ☏5323-3460; http://tokyo. park.hyatt.jp/en/hotel/dining/Kozue.html; 40th fl, Park Hyatt, 3-7-1-2 Nishi-Shinjuku, Shinjuku-ku; lunch/dinner courses from ¥2700/15,000; ⏰11.30am-2.30pm & 5.30-9.30pm; ⓢŌedo line to Tochōmae, exit A4)

Omoide-yokochō

YAKITORI $

7 Map p100, C2

Since the postwar days, smoke has been billowing night and day from the *yakitori* stalls that line this alley by the train tracks, literally translated as 'Memory Lane', and less politely known as Shonben-yokochō (Piss Alley). Several stalls have English menus. (思い出横丁; Nishi-Shinjuku 1-chōme, Shinjuku-ku; skewers from ¥100; ⏰noon-midnight, hours vary by shop; ⓡJR Yamanote line to Shinjuku, west exit)

Numazukō

SUSHI $

8 Map p100, B3

Shinjuku's best *kaiten-sushi* (conveyor-belt sushi) restaurant has a long, snaking counter and a huge menu; it's pricier than most but the quality is worth it. It's below the Shinjuku Highway Bus Terminal, two basement floors down. You can also get there via an underground passage

Understand

Tokyo Today

Tokyo has reinvented itself countless times in the four centuries since its founding. With the 2020 Summer Olympic Games on the horizon, it hopes to do so again, with plans for a greener, friendlier city.

Tokyo Vision 2020

Since it was announced in 2013 that Tokyo would hold the 2020 Summer Olympics, the city has gone into full preparation mode, enacting its 'Tokyo Vision 2020'. The 1964 Tokyo Summer Olympics – the first to be held in Asia – marked Tokyo's big comeback after the city was all but destroyed in WWII. The powers that be are hoping that the 2020 games will again be symbolic, reaffirming Tokyo's position in the pantheon of world's great cities following more than two decades of economic malaise.

 The most dramatic redevelopment will take place along Tokyo Bay, where many of the events will be held. Already in the works (and set to be completed in 2016) is the Umi-no-Mori (Sea Forest), a vast green space on one of the bay's human-made landfill islands. Other positive changes to look forward to: expanded wireless networks and increased flight capacity for Haneda, Tokyo's more convenient airport. Private developers will no doubt seek to ride the Olympic wave as well, meaning even more construction projects. One controversial idea that has been bandied around: allowing casinos.

City of the Future

Something else noteworthy is slated to happen in 2020: while the population of Japan has been dropping off since 2004, it's predicted that Tokyo's population will peak at 13.35 million in 2020 and then also begin to decline. The birth rate for the capital hovers around 1.1 (even lower than the national average of 1.4). Tokyo is seen as a forerunner – facing the kinds of problems that cities around the world will face in the future, as their populations begin a similar tapering off. The city's Tokyo Vision 2020 also includes provisions for making Tokyo a more attractive city in which to work: for example, more childcare facilities, job centres for senior citizens and special economic zones for foreign companies. If it works, Tokyo could become a model for cities of the future.

Top Tip

Picnic in the Park

The grassy lawns at Shinjuku-gyoen (p101) are perfect for a picnic. Pick up a *bentō* (boxed meal) from the *depachika* (department store food floor) at Isetan (p107) or a convenience store on the way.

from Shinjuku Station; look for the fish-shaped sign over the door. (沼津港; Basement, My Bldg, 1-10-1 Nishi-Shinjuku, Shinjuku-ku; plates ¥90-550; ⏱11am-10.30pm; 🚃JR Yamanote line to Shinjuku, west exit)

Shinjuku Asia-yokochō ASIAN $

 9 🍴 Map p100, C1

A rooftop night market that spans the Asian continent, Asia-yokochō has vendors dishing out everything from Korean *bibimbap* to Vietnamese *pho*. It's noisy, a bit chaotic and particularly fun in a group. (新宿アジア横丁; Rooftop, 2nd Toa Hall Bldg, 1-21-1 Kabukichō, Shinjuku-ku; dishes from ¥650; ⏱5pm-5am; 🚃JR Yamanote line to Shinjuku, east exit)

Tsunahachi TEMPURA $$

10 🍴 Map p100, D2

Tsunahachi has been expertly frying prawns and seasonal vegetables for nearly 90 years. The sets are served in courses so each dish comes piping hot. Sit at the counter for the added pleasure of watching the chefs at work. Indigo *noren* (curtains) mark the entrance. (つな八; ☎3352-1012; www.tunahachi.co.jp;

3-31-8 Shinjuku, Shinjuku-ku; lunch/dinner from ¥1296-2268; ⏱11am-10.30pm; 🚃JR Yamanote line to Shinjuku, east exit)

Tsuki no Shizuka IZAKAYA $$

11 🍴 Map p100, B2

This lively, popular *izakaya* (Japanese pub-eatery) makes ordering easy and fun, with tableside touch-screen devices (in English). Look for staples, such as *kara-age* (fried chicken), sashimi, and *goma-dōfu* (sesame tofu). There's a glowing sign over the stairs. (月ノ雫; www.tsukino-shizuka.com; 2nd & 3rd fl, 1-12-1 Nishi-Shinjuku, Shinjuku-ku; dishes ¥480-980; ⏱11.30am-2pm, 5pm-midnight Mon-Thurs, to 5am Fri, 4pm-5am Sat, 4pm-midnight Sun; 📷; 🚃JR Yamanote line to Shinjuku, west exit)

Drinking

Zoetrope BAR

12 🍷 Map p100, C1

A must visit for whisky fans, Zoetrope has no less than 300 varieties of Japanese whisky (from ¥700) behind its small counter – including some no longer commercially available. The owner speaks some English and can help you pick from the daunting menu. He'll also let you choose the soundtrack to play alongside the silent films he screens on the wall. (ゾートロープ; http://homepage2.nifty.com/zoetrope; 3rd fl, 7-10-14 Nishi-Shinjuku, Shinjuku-ku; ⏱7pm-4am Mon-Sat; 🚃JR Yamanote line to Shinjuku, west exit)

A tiny bar in Golden Gai (p99)

Advocates Café
GAY & LESBIAN

13 Map p100, E2

The scene at this tiny, teeny corner bar overflows onto the street and becomes more like a block party, especially in the summer. Advocates has a popular happy hour – 'beer blast' (all you can drink for ¥1000; 6–9pm) – and is a great place to start the evening, meet new people and find out where the next party is. It's open to all; staff speak English. (アドボケイツカフェ; http://advocates-cafe.com; 2-18-1 Shinjuku, Shinjuku-ku; ⏰6pm-4am, to 1am Sun; Ⓢ Marunouchi line to Shinjuku-sanchōme, exit C8)

Samurai
BAR

14 Map p100, C2

Never mind the impeccable record collection, this eccentric jazz *kissa* (cafe where jazz records are played) is worth a visit just for the owner's impressive collection of 2500 *maneki-neko* (beckoning cats). Look for the sign next door to Disc Union and take the elevator. There's a ¥300 cover charge (¥500 after 9pm); drinks from ¥650. (サムライ; http://jazz-samurai.see-saa.net; 5th fl, 3-35-5 Shinjuku, Shinjuku-ku; ⏰6pm-1am; ℞ JR Yamanote line to Shinjuku, southeast exit)

Understand
Karaoke

- -

Karaoke (カラオケ; pronounced kah-rah-oh-kay) isn't just about singing: it's an excuse to let loose, a bonding ritual, a reason to keep the party going past the last train and a way to kill time until the first one starts in the morning. When words fail, it's a way to express yourself – are you the type to sing the latest J-pop hit (dance moves included) or do you go in for an Okinawan folk ballad? It doesn't matter if you're a good singer or not (though the tone-deaf might sign up for singing lessons – such is the important social function of karaoke), as long as you've got heart.

In Japan, karaoke is sung in a private room among friends. Admission is usually charged per person per half-hour. Food and drinks (ordered by phone) are brought to the room. To choose a song, use the touch screen device to search by artist or title; most have an English function and plenty of English songs to choose from. Then let your inner diva shine. Shinjuku has branches of major chains like Karaoke-kan (カラオケ館) and Big Echo (ビッグエコー).

New York Bar
BAR

15 Map p100, A4

You may not be lodging at the Park Hyatt, but you can still ascend to the 52nd floor to swoon over the nightscape from the floor-to-ceiling windows at this bar (of *Lost in Translation* fame). There's a cover charge of ¥2200 after 8pm (7pm Sunday) and live music nightly; cocktails start at ¥1800. Note: the dress code is enforced. (ニューヨークバー; ☎5323-3458; http://tokyo.park.hyatt.com; 52nd fl, Park Hyatt, 3-7-1-2 Nishi-Shinjuku, Shinjuku-ku; ⏰5pm-midnight Sun-Wed, to 1am Thu-Sat; Ⓜ Ōedo line to Tochōmae, exit A4)

Arty Farty
GAY & LESBIAN

16 Map p100, D2

A fixture on Tokyo's gay scene for many a moon, Arty Farty welcomes all in the community to come shake a tail feather on the dance floor here. It usually gets going later in the evening. (アーティファーティ; www.arty-farty.net; 2nd fl, 2-11-7 Shinjuku, Shinjuku-ku; ⏰6pm-1am; Ⓢ Marunouchi line to Shinjuku-sanchōme, exit C8)

Entertainment

Robot Restaurant
CABARET

17 ⭐ Map p100, D1

This Kabukichō spectacle is wacky Japan at its finest, with giant robots manned by bikini-clad women and enough neon to light all of Shinjuku. It's equal part girlie show (but no nudity) and hilarity. Reservations recommended, but not necessary. Look for discount tickets in free

English-language mags around town. (ロボットレストラン; ☎3200-5500; www.robot-restaurant.com; 1-7-1 Kabukichō, Shinjuku-ku; tickets ¥7000; ⊗shows at 4pm, 5.55pm, 7.50pm & 9.45pm; 🚈JR Yamanote line to Shinjuku, east exit)

Shinjuku Pit Inn JAZZ

 18 Map p100, D2

This is not the kind of place you come to talk over the music. Aficionados have been coming here for more than 40 years to listen to Japan's best jazz performers. Weekday matinées feature new artists and cost only ¥1300. (新宿ピットイン; ☎3354-2024; www.pit-inn.com; Basement, 2-12-4 Shinjuku, Shinjuku-ku; admission from ¥3000; ⊗matinée 2.30pm, evening show 7.30pm; Ⓢ Marunouchi line to Shinjuku-sanchōme, exit C5)

Shopping

Isetan DEPARTMENT STORE

 19 Map p100, D2

Most department stores play to conservative tastes, but not this one. Women can head to the Re-Style section on the 2nd floor for up-and-coming Japanese designers. Men get a whole building of their own (connected by a passageway). Don't miss the basement food hall, featuring some of the country's top purveyors of sweet and savoury goodies. (伊勢丹; www.isetan.co.jp; 3-14-1 Shinjuku, Shinjuku-ku; ⊗10am-8pm; Ⓢ Marunouchi line to Shinjuku-sanchōme, exits B3, B4 & B5)

RanKing RanQueen VARIETY

 20 Map p100, C2

If it's trendy, it's here. This clever shop stocks only the top-selling products in any given category, from eyeliner and soft drinks to leg-slimming massage rollers. Look for it just outside the east-exit ticket gates of JR Shinjuku Station. (ランキンランキン; Basement, Shinjuku Station, Shinjuku-ku; ⊗10am-11pm; 🚈JR Yamanote line to Shinjuku, east exit)

Disk Union MUSIC

 21 Map p100, D2

Scruffy Disk Union is known by local audiophiles as Tokyo's best used CD and vinyl store. Eight storeys carry a variety of musical styles; if you still can't find what you're looking for, there are several other branches in Shinjuku that stock more obscure genres (pick up a map here). (ディスクユニオン; 3-31-4 Shinjuku, Shinjuku-ku; ⊗11am-9pm; 🚈JR Yamanote line to Shinjuku, east exit)

Bicqlo CLOTHING, ELECTRONICS

 22 Map p100, D2

This mash-up store brings two of Japan's favourite retailers – electronics outfitter Bic Camera and budget clothing chain Uniqlo – under one roof. So you can match your new camera to your new hoodie. It's bright white: you can't miss it. (ビックロ; 3-29-1 Shinjuku, Shinjuku-ku; ⊗10am-10pm; Ⓢ Marunouchi line to Shinjuku-sanchōme, exit A5)

Top Sights
Ghibli Museum

Getting There

🚈 **Train** Take a JR Chūō line train from Shinjuku to Mitaka. From the number 9 bus stop at the south exit, get a shuttle bus (round trip/one way ¥320/210, every 20 minutes) for the museum.

From 1986 until his retirement in 2014, master animator Miyazaki Hayao and his Studio Ghibli (pronounced 'jiburi') were responsible for some of the best-loved films in Japan – and the world. The most wellknown is the Academy Award–winning *Spirited Away* (2001). Miyazaki designed this museum himself, and it's redolent of the fairy-tale atmosphere that makes his animations so enchanting. The only catch: tickets must be purchased in advance, and you must choose the exact time and date you plan to visit.

Ghibli Museum

Don't Miss

The Theatre

An original 20-minute animated short film plays in a small, whimsically decorated theatre inside the museum (you'll get a ticket for this when you enter). It changes every season to keep fans coming back.

The Robot Soldier

Head up to the rooftop terrace – a delight in warmer weather – to see the 5m-tall sculpture of the robot soldier from the early Miyazaki film *Laputa* (1986).

The Catbus

Even if your kids haven't seen the Studio Ghibli classic *My Neighbor Totoro* (1988), they'll love the giant plush cat bus that they can climb on. Sorry, grown-ups: this one is for under 12s only.

Getting Tickets

Purchase tickets online through a travel agent before you arrive in Japan or from a kiosk at any Lawson convenience store in Tokyo (the trickier option, as it will require some Japanese-language ability to navigate the ticket machine). Both options are explained in detail on the website.

Nearby: Inokashira-kōen

The Ghibli Museum is actually in the corner of one of Tokyo's best parks, **Inokashira-kōen** (井の頭公園; www.kensetsu.metro.tokyo.jp/seibuk/inokashira/index.html; 1-18-31 Gotenyama, Musashino-shi; 🚉JR Chūō line to Kichijōji, Kōen exit). Instead of heading back to Mitaka Station, walk through the park to Kichijōji Station (also on the JR Chūō line). The walk takes about 30 minutes. Along the way you'll pass a big pond with an island where an ancient shrine to the sea goddess Benzaiten stands.

ジブリ美術館

www.ghibli-museum.jp

1-1-83 Shimo-Renjaku, Mitaka-shi

adult ¥1000, child ¥100-700

🕐10am-6pm Wed-Mon

🚉JR Chūō line to Mitaka, south exit

☑ Top Tips

▶ Tickets are limited and go fast (especially during the summer holiday). You can buy them up to three months in advance from a travel agent.

▶ Download a map from the website.

✕ Take a Break

After the museum, walk through Inokashira-kōen and stop for Thai at **Pepa Cafe Forest** (ペパカフェフォレスト; www.peppermintcafe.com/forest; 4-1-5 Inokashira, Mitaka-shi; 🕐noon-10pm; 🚉JR Chūō line to Kichijōji, Kōen exit), in the park. The museum also has a cafe that serves lunches made with organic veggies.

Explore

Kōrakuen & Around

Northwest of the Imperial Palace, Kōrakuen is off the major tourist trail, yet has a number of fascinating sights. These include the landscaped garden Koishikawa Kōrakuen and the controversial shrine Yasukuni-jinja. Nearby Kagurazaka, an old geisha district now resplendent with shops and cafes, is a wonderful place to wander. And baseball fans will not want to miss the spectacle at Tokyo Dome.

The Sights in a Day

☀ Start the day with a visit to the garden **Koishikawa Kōrakuen** (p113), to enjoy the early-morning light through the leaves. Then stroll over to **Canal Cafe** (p116), for an alfresco lunch along the outer moat of the Imperial Palace.

☼ After lunch, head down to the shrine to Japan's war dead, **Yasukuni-jinja** (p113). You'll pass another shrine, **Tokyo Dai-jingū** (p114), on the way too. To learn more about Japan's wartime history, you can visit the controversial **Yūshū-kan** (p113), a war museum with a particular view of history, or the **National Shōwa Memorial Museum** (p113), which depicts the life of ordinary Japanese during WWII. Alternatively, head up the hill to **Kagurazaka** (p115) and wander the neighbourhood's atmospheric cobblestone streets.

☾ In the evening, during the warmer months, you can catch a baseball game at **Tokyo Dome** (p115). Another option is to unwind in the hotspring pools at **Spa LaQua** (p113). For dinner, **Kado** (p115), which specialises in traditional Japanese home cooking, is highly recommended. The restaurant is in Kagurazaka, where you'll find a number of small cafes and bars, like **Beer Bar Bitter** (p116).

 Best of Tokyo

Temples & Shrines
Yasukuni-jinja (p113)

Parks & Gardens
Koishikawa Kōrakuen (p113)

Galleries & Museums
National Shōwa Memorial Museum (p113)

Food
Kado (p115)

Sentō & Onsen
Spa LaQua (p113)

Getting There

🚃 **Train** The JR Sōbu line stops at Iidabashi. Rapid-service JR Chūō line trains, which use the same track, skip Iidabashi but stop at Suidōbashi.

Ⓢ **Subway** The Tōzai line is the most convenient, stopping at Kagurazaka, Iidabashi, Kudanshita and Takebashi. The Ōedo, Yūrakuchō and Namboku lines also stop at Iidabashi; the Hanzōmon line stops at Kudanshita and Jimbōchō.

BUNKYŌ-KU

HONGŌ

Sotobori-dōri

Kanda-gawa

KANDA-JIMBŌCHŌ

S Takebashi

S Suidōbashi

Jimbōchō S

Suzuran-dōri

Hakusan-dōri

Spa 2 ⊙
LaQua

6 ⊙
Tokyo
Dome City
Attractions

MISAKI-CHŌ

Suidōbashi Ⓢ

KŌRAKU

Mejiro-dōri

S Kudanshita

Tokyo 9 ⊙
Dome

4 ⊙

Kitanomaru-kōen

Koishikawa 1 ⊙
Kōrakuen

Shuto Expwy No 5

IIDABASHI

Nihombashi-gawa

National Shōwa
Memorial
Museum

Uchibori-dōri

S Iidabashi

Iidabashi S

Tokyo 8 ⊙
Dai-jingū

FUJIMI

Yūsha- 5 ⊙
kan

Indian Ⓗ
Embassy

KUDAN-MINAMI

Iidabashi Ⓢ

Iidabashi Ⓢ

19 ⓐ

13 ⓐ

AKAGI-MOTOMACHI

Ōkubo-dōri

15 ⓐ

18 ⓐ

TSUKUDO-CHŌ

Kagurazaka-dōri

11 ⓑ

14 ⓐ

17 ⓐ

KAGURAZAKA

Hyōgo-yokochō

Sotobori-dōri

WAKAMIYA-CHŌ

Mizuma Art 7 ⊙
Gallery

12 ⓧ

Yasukuni-jinja 3 ⊙

KUDANKITA

Yasukuni-dōri

Ⓢ Ushigome-kagurazaka

10 ⓧ

16 ⓐ

Waseda-dōri

SHINJUKU-KU

S Kagurazaka

Ōkubo-dōri

ICHIGAYA-TAMACHI

Sotobori Moat

Ⓜ Ichigaya

Ⓢ Ichigaya

Ichigaya Ⓢ

Ⓢ Ichigaya

400 m
0.2 miles

Ⓝ

Sights

Koishikawa Kōrakuen   GARDENS

1 ◎ Map p112, D1

Established in the mid-17th century as the property of the Tokugawa clan, this formal strolling garden incorporates elements of Chinese and Japanese landscaping. It's among Tokyo's most attractive gardens, although nowadays the *shakkei* (borrowed scenery) also includes the other-worldly Tokyo Dome. Don't miss the Engetsu-kyō (Full-Moon Bridge), which dates from the early Edo period. (小石川後楽園; 1-6-6 Kōraku, Bunkyō-ku; adult/child ¥300/free; ◉9am-5pm; ®JR Sōbu line to Iidabashi, exit C3)

Spa LaQua   ONSEN

2 ◎ Map p112, D1

One of Tokyo's few true onsen, this chic spa complex relies on natural hot-spring water from 1700m below ground. There are indoor and outdoor baths, saunas and add-on options, such as *akasuri* (Korean-style whole-body exfoliation). It's a fascinating introduction to Japanese health and beauty rituals. (スパ ラクーア; www.laqua.jp; 5th-9th fl, Tokyo Dome City, 1-3-61 Kōraku, Bunkyō-ku; admission weekday/weekend ¥2634/2958; ◉11am-9pm; ⑤Marunouchi line to Kōrakuen, exit 2)

Yasukuni-jinja   SHINTO SHRINE

3 ◎ Map p112, B4

Literally 'For the Peace of the Country Shrine', Yasukuni is the memorial shrine to Japan's war dead, around 2.5 million souls. Completed in 1869, it has unusual *torii* (gates) made of steel and bronze. It is also incredibly controversial: in 1978 14 class-A war criminals, including WWII general Hideki Tōjō, were enshrined here. (靖国神社; ☎3261-8326; www.yasukuni.or.jp; 3-1-1 Kudan-kita, Chiyoda-ku; ◉6am-5pm; ⑤Hanzōmon line to Kudanshita, exit 1)

National Shōwa Memorial Museum   MUSEUM

4 ◎ Map p112, D3

This museum of WWII-era Tokyo gives a sense of everyday life for the common people: how they ate, slept, dressed, studied, prepared for war and endured martial law, famine and loss of loved ones. An English audio guide (free) fills in a lot. (昭和館; Shōwa-kan; ☎3222-2577; www.showakan.go.jp; 1-6-1 Kudan-minami, Chiyoda-ku; adult/student/child ¥300/150/80; ◉10am-5.30pm; ®Hanzōmon line to Kudanshita, exit 4)

Yūshū-kan   MUSEUM

5 ◎ Map p112, B3

Most history museums in Japan skirt the issue of war or focus on the burden of the common people. Not so here: Yūshū-kan begins with Japan's samurai tradition and ends with its defeat in WWII. It is also unapologetic and has been known to boil the blood of some visitors with its particular view of history. (遊就館; ☎3261-8326; www.yasukuni.or.jp; 3-1-1 Kudankita, Chiyoda-ku; adult/student ¥800/500; ◉9am-4pm; ⑤Hanzōmon line to Kudanshita, exit 1)

Understand
The Yasukuni Controversy

Yasukuni-jinja (p113) was erected by the Meiji government to honour those who died bringing about the Meiji Restoration. Since then, it has become a shrine to all war casualties, including enlisted men, civilians and, since 1978, 14 class-A war criminals, among them WWII general Hideki Tōjō – hence the controversy.

Following the separation of religion and state in 1946 enacted by the American occupation, management of Yasukuni-jinja was transferred to a private religious organisation. Still, leading politicians occasionally visit the shrine to pay their respects, most often on the anniversary of the end of WWII. This angers Japan's Asian neighbours, who suffered greatly in Japan's wars of expansion of the 20th century. As a result, the decision by a sitting prime minister to visit the shrine or not is seen as a strong political statement, and is watched throughout East Asia. No emperor has visited Yasukuni-jinja since 1978.

Tokyo Dome City Attractions
AMUSEMENT PARK

6 ◉ Map p112, D1

The top attraction at this amusement park next to Tokyo Dome is the 'Thunder Dolphin' (¥1030), a roller coaster that cuts a heart-in-your-throat course in and around the tightly packed buildings of downtown. There are plenty of low-key, child-friendly rides as well. You can buy tickets for individual rides or a day pass (adult/child ¥3900/2100; after 5pm adult ¥2900). (東京ドームシティアトラクションズ; ☑3817-6001; www.tokyo-dome.co.jp/e; 1-3-61 Kōraku, Bunkyō-ku; attractions ¥420-1030; ◷10am-9pm; Ⓡ JR Chūō line to Suidōbashi, west exit)

Mizuma Art Gallery
GALLERY

7 ◉ Map p112, B3

Run by longtime Tokyo art-world figure Sueo Mizuma, Mizuma Art Gallery represents some of Japan's more successful contemporary artists, such as Aida Makoto and Konoike Tomoko. Shows often feature *neo-nihonga* (Japanese-style paintings with contemporary panache). It's in a metal building above a small parking lot. (www.mizuma-art.co.jp; 2nd fl, 3-13 Ichigaya-tamachi, Shinjuku-ku; ◷11am-7pm Tue-Sat; Ⓡ JR Sōbu line to Ichigaya, exit 1)

Tokyo Dai-jingū
SHINTO SHRINE

8 ◉ Map p112, C2

This is the Tokyo branch of Ise-jingū, Japan's mother shrine in Mie prefecture. Credited with establishing the Shintō wedding ritual, Tokyo Dai-jingū is a popular pilgrimage site for young Tokyoites hoping to get hitched and does a brisk business in marriage charms. (東京大神宮; ☑3262-3566; www.tokyodaijingu.or.jp/english; 2-4-1 Fujimi, Chiyoda-ku; ◷6am-9pm; Ⓡ JR Sōbu line to Iidabashi, west exit)

Tokyo Dome

BASEBALL

9 Map p112, D1

Tokyo Dome (aka 'Big Egg') is home to the Yomiuri Giants. Love 'em or hate 'em, they're the most consistently successful team in Japanese baseball. If you're looking to see the Giants in action, the baseball season runs from the end of March to the end of October. Tickets sell out in advance; get them early at www.giants.jp/en. (東京ドーム; www.tokyo-dome.co.jp/e; 1-3 Kōraku, Bunkyō-ku; tickets ¥2200-6100; ⊠JR Chūō line to Suidōbashi, west exit)

Eating

Kado

JAPANESE $$

10 Map p112, A1

Set in an old wooden house, Kado specialises in *katei-ryōri* (home cooking). Dinner is a set course of seasonal dishes (such as grilled quail or crab soup). At lunch there's no English menu, so your best bet is the カド定食 (*kado teishoku*), the daily house special. Bookings are required for dinner; the restaurant has a wooden facade and a white lantern out front. (カド; ⊠3268-2410; http://kagurazaka-kado.com; 1-32 Akagi-Motomachi, Shinjuku-ku; lunch/dinner sets from ¥800/3150; ⊙11.30am-2.30pm & 5-11pm; ⊠Tōzai line to Kagurazaka, exit 1)

Le Bretagne

FRENCH $

11 Map p112, B2

This French-owned cafe, hidden on a cobblestone lane in Kagurazaka, is credited with starting the Japanese rage for crêpes. Savoury buckwheat galettes are made with ham and cheese imported from France; the sweet ones – served with the likes of caramelised butter, apple compote and ice cream – are divine. (ル ブル ターニュ; ⊠3235-3001; www.le-bretagne. com/e/top.html; 4-2 Kagurazaka, Shinjuku-ku; crêpes ¥750-1850; ⊙11.30am-10.30pm Tue-Sat, to 10pm Sun; ⊠JR Sōbu line to Iidabashi, west exit)

Kururi

RĀMEN $

12 Map p112, B3

The line-up of *rāmen* fanatics outside this cramped, anonymous noodle shop proves its street cred. The *miso-rāmen* (みそらぁめん) broth is swamp-thick,

---

Understand

Kagurazaka

In the beginning of the 20th century, Kagurazaka was a fashionable *hanamachi* – a pleasure quarter where geisha entertained. Though the geisha have disappeared, the neighbourhood retains the glamour and charm of decades past, with winding cobblestone streets and cosy cafes. To access the most enchanting backstreets, walk from Iidabashi Station up Kagurazaka Hill and turn right at the Royal Host restaurant. Don't miss Hyogo-yokochō, the neighbourhood's oldest lane and its most atmospheric – it's often used in television and movie shoots.

incredibly rich and delicious. There's no sign, but it's next to a liquor shop with a striped awning; buy a ticket inside from the machine. (麺処くるり; 3-2 Ichigaya-Tamachi, Shinjuku; noodles ¥700-950; ⏰11am-9pm; 🚃JR Sōbu line to Iidabashi, west exit)

Canal Cafe
ITALIAN **$$**

13 Map p112, B2

Along the languid moat that forms the edge of Kitanomaru-kōen, this is one of Tokyo's best alfresco dining spots. The restaurant serves tasty wood-fired pizzas, seafood pastas and grilled meats, while over on the 'deck side' you can settle in with a sandwich, muffin or a cup of coffee. (カナルカフェ; 📞3260-8068; www.canalcafe.jp; 1-9 Kagurazaka, Shinjuku-ku; lunch from ¥1600, dinner mains ¥1500-2800; ⏰11.30am-11pm Tue-Sat, to 9.30pm Sun; 🖊; 🚃JR Sōbu line to Iidabashi, west exit)

Local Life
Book Town Jimbōchō

Jimbōchō is home to more than 100 secondhand bookshops, and it's a favourite destination for local bibliophiles. Worth a visit is **Ohya Shobō** (大屋書房; 📞3291-0062; www.ohya-shobo.com; 1-1 Kanda-Jimbōchō, Chiyoda-ku; ⏰10am-6pm Mon-Sat; 🚃Hanzōmon line to Jimbōchō, exit A7), a splendid, musty old bookshop that specialises in *ukiyo-e* (wood-block prints), vintage (Edo-era) manga, and antique maps. It's a two-minute walk east of Jimbōchō station along Yasukuni-dōri.

Drinking

Mugimaru 2
CAFE

14 Map p112, B2

This old house, almost completely covered in ivy, is a favourite local hang-out. Seating is on floor cushions; warm, squishy *manjū* (steamed buns) are the house speciality. It's inside a tangle of alleys just off of Ōkubo-dōri; look for a sign with a cat and potted plants out front. (ムギマル2; 📞5228-6393; www.mugimaru2.com; 5-20 Kagurazaka, Shinjuku-ku; coffee ¥550; ⏰noon-9pm Thu-Tue; 🚇Tozai line to Kagurazaka, exit 1)

Beer Bar Bitter
BAR

15 Map p112, B2

This Kagurazaka hideaway has Belgian beer on tap and a moody, industrial interior. Look for it above a bistro called Viande and take the stairs on the right. (ビアバービター; 📞5261-3087; www.beerbar-bitter.com; 2nd fl, 1-14 Tsukudochō, Shinjuku-ku; ⏰5pm-2am Sun-Fri; 🚃JR Sōbu line to Iidabashi, west exit)

Shopping

Baikatei
FOOD

16 Map p112, A1

See (and sample) humble beans and rice whipped into pastel flowers at this award-winning traditional sweets shop, in business since 1935. There are blue door curtains out front. (梅花亭; 6-15 Kagurazaka, Shinjuku-ku; ⏰10am-8pm; 🚇Tōzai line to Kagurazaka, exit 1)

GREG ELMS/GETTY IMAGES ©

Tokyo Dome (p115)

La Ronde D'Argile
HOMEWARES

17 🔒 Map p112, B2

A changing selection of homewares made by local artisans fill two floors of this old house turned shop. It has a picture window out front, with a small stained-glass sign above it. (ラ・ロンダジル; 📞3260-6801; http://la-ronde.com; 11 Wakamiya-chō, Shinjuku-ku; ⏰11.30am-6pm Tue-Sat; Ⓢ Ōedo line to Ushigome-Kagurazaka, exit A2)

Kukuli
CRAFTS

18 🔒 Map p112, B2

One of several shops in Kagurazaka specialising in traditional craftwork. Here it's hand-dyed textiles (such as scarves and tea towels) with a modern touch. (www.kukuli.co.jp; 1-10 Tsukudo-chō, Shinjuku-ku; ⏰11am-7pm; 🚉JR Yamanote line to Iidabashi, west exit)

Puppet House
CRAFTS

19 🔒 Map p112, C2

Japan's only dedicated puppet shop is a showcase for one-of-a-kind handmade marionettes from around the world. It's obviously a labour of love and the English-speaking owner is happy to show you how to make the puppets walk, skip and dance. Look for the sign of Punch at the entrance to an alley. (パペットハウス; www.puppet-house.co.jp; 1-8 Shimomiyabi-chō, Shinjuku-ku; ⏰11am-7pm Tue-Sat; 🚉JR Sōbu line to Iidabashi, east exit)

Local Life
An Afternoon in Akihabara

Getting There

🚃 **Train** The JR Yamanote and Sōbu lines stop at Akihabara; Electric Town exit is the most convenient.

S **Subway** The Hibiya line stops at Akihabara; take exit 3.

Akihabara ('Akiba' to friends) is the centre of Tokyo's *otaku* (geek) subculture. But you don't have to obsess about manga (Japanese comics) or anime (Japanese animation) to enjoy this quirky neighbourhood. It's equal parts sensory overload and cultural mind-bender. In fact, as the *otaku* subculture gains more and more influence on the culture at large, Akiba is drawing more visitors who don't fit the stereotype.

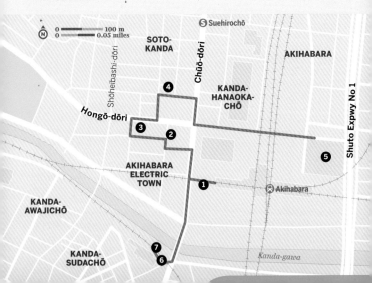

1 Explore 'Electric Town'

Before Akihabara became *otaku*-land, it was Electric Town – the place for discounted electronics and where early computer geeks tracked down obscure parts for home-built machines. **Akihabara Radio Center** (秋葉原ラジオセンター; 1-14-2 Soto-Kanda, Chiyoda-ku; ⏰hours vary; 🚆JR Yamanote line to Akihabara, Electric Town exit), a warren of stalls under the train tracks, keeps the tradition alive.

2 Play Vintage Arcade Games

In Akihabara, a love of the new is tempered with a deep affection for the old. **Super Potato Retro-kan** (スーパーポテトレトロ館; www.superpotato.com; 1-11-2 Soto-kanda, Chiyoda-ku; ⏰11am-8pm Mon-Fri, from 10am Sat & Sun; 🚆JR Yamanote line to Akihabara, Electric Town exit) is a retro video arcade with some old-school consoles.

3 Visit a Maid Cafe

Maid cafes – where waitresses dress as French maids and treat customers with giggling deference to *go-shujinsama* (master) – are an Akiba institution. Pop into **@Home** (@ほぉ～むカフェ; www.cafe-athome.com; 4th-7th fl, 1-11-4 Soto-Kanda, Chiyoda-ku; drinks from ¥500; ⏰11.30am-10pm Mon-Fri, 10.30am-10pm Sat & Sun; 🚆JR Yamanote line to Akihabara, Electric Town exit) for a game of *moe moe jankan* (rock, paper, scissors) maid-style.

4 Shop at Mandarake Complex

To get an idea of what *otaku* obsess over, a trip to **Mandarake Complex** (まんだらけコンプレックス; www.mandarake.co.jp; 3-11-2 Soto-Kanda, Chiyoda-ku; ⏰noon-8pm; 🚆JR Yamanote line to Akihabara, Electric Town exit) will do the trick. It's eight storeys of comic books and DVDs, action figures and cel art.

5 Pop into Yodobashi Akiba

The modern avatar of Akihabara Radio Center is **Yodobashi Akiba** (ヨドバシカメラ Akiba; www.yodobashi-akiba.com; 1-1 Kanda Hanaoka-chō, Chiyoda-ku; ⏰9.30am-10pm; 🚆JR Yamanote line to Akihabara, Shōwa-tōriguchi exit), a monster electronics store beloved by camera junkies. But for all the modern conveniences Yodobashi Akiba feels like an old-time bazaar.

6 Check out an Old Train Station

MAAch ecute (www.maach-ecute.jp; 1-25-4 Kanda-Sudachō, Chiyoda-ku; ⏰11am-9pm Mon-Sat, to 8pm Sun; 🚆Chūo or Sōbu lines to Akihabara, Electric Town exit) is a shopping and dining complex, crafted from the old station and railway arches of Mansei-bashi, selling homewares, fashion and foods from around Japan.

7 Visit a Trainspotters' Cafe

While mAAch ecute mall may have little to do with *otaku* sensibilities, cafe **N3331** (📞5295-2788; http://n3331.com; 2nd fl, mAAch ecute 1-25-4 Kanda-Sudachō, Chiyoda-ku; ⏰11am-10.30pm Mon-Sat, to 8.30pm Sun; 🚆JR Yamamote line to Akihabara, Electric Town exit), on the 2nd floor, will appeal to *densha otaku* (train geeks). From floor-to-ceiling windows, watch commuter trains stream by while sipping on coffee, craft beer or sake.

Explore

Ueno

Ueno is the cultural heart of Tokyo and has been the city's top tourist draw for centuries. At the centre of the neighbourhood is a sprawling park, Ueno-kōen, home to numerous museums, including Japan's grandest, the Tokyo National Museum. There are also temples, shrines, century-old restaurants and an open-air market – all of which lend Ueno a classic, traditional atmosphere.

The Sights in a Day

Start the morning with a visit to the **Tokyo National Museum** (p122), giving yourself two hours to explore the highlights of the museum's vast collection of Japanese art and antiquities. Get tea at **Torindō** (p130), then stroll through leafy **Ueno-kōen** (p127), with its shrines and temples, such as **Kiyōmizu Kannon-dō** (p127) and **Ueno Tōshō-gū** (p127). Break for lunch at historic **Izu-ei** (p130), which specialises in barbecued eel – a classic Japanese dish.

After lunch take your pick from some of the excellent smaller museums: the **Shitamachi Museum** (p128), for a taste of prewar Tokyo; the **National Science Museum** (p129), for the low-down on the local flora and fauna; the **Kyū Iwasaki-teien** (p128), for a glimpse into the life of the late-19th-century elite; or the **Yokoyama Taikan Memorial Hall** (p128), for a look into an artist's life in the early 20th century. When the museums close, take a walk through the old-fashioned arcade, **Ameya-yokochō** (p127).

In the evening head to **Shinsuke** (p129), one of Tokyo's best *izakaya* (Japanese pub-eateries).

For a local's afternoon in Yanaka, see p124.

 Top Sights

Tokyo National Museum (p122)

Local Life

An Afternoon in Historic Yanaka (p124)

Best of Ueno

Architecture
Kyū Iwasaki-teien (p128)

Temples & Shrines
Kiyōmizu Kannon-dō (p127)

Ueno Tōshō-gū (p127)

Parks & Gardens
Ueno-kōen (p127)

Galleries & Museums
SCAI the Bathhouse (p125)

Food
Shinsuke (p129)

Getting There

Train The JR Yamanote line stops at Ueno, Nippori and Nishi-Nippori. Keisei line trains for Narita Airport leave from Keisei Ueno Station.

S Subway The Hibiya and Ginza lines stop at Ueno. The Chiyoda line stops at Yushima, Nezu, Sendagi and Nishi-Nippori.

Top Sights
Tokyo National Museum

The world's largest collection of Japanese art covers ancient pottery, religious sculpture, samurai swords, *ukiyo-e* (wood-block prints), exquisite kimonos, and much, much more. There are several buildings, the most important of which is the Honkan (Main or Japan Gallery). Exhibitions here are designed to give visitors an overview of Japanese art history throughout the last few millennia. Other highlights include 7th-century Buddhist relics inside the Gallery of Hōryū-ji Treasures and the Asian artefacts in the Tōyōkan (Gallery of Eastern Antiquities).

東京国立博物館, Tokyo Kokuritsu Hakubutsukan

👁 Map p126, C3

📞 3822-1111

www.tnm.jp

13-9 Ueno-kōen, Taitō-ku

🚉 JR Yamanote line to Ueno, Ueno-kōen exit

Wood-block prints at Tokyo National Museum

Don't Miss

National Treasure Gallery

A single, superlative work from the museum's collection of 88 National Treasures – perhaps a painted screen, or a gilded, hand-drawn *sutra* (Buddhist scripture) – is displayed here in a serene, contemplative setting. (Honkan Room 2)

Art of the Imperial Court

The poetry scrolls and ornately decorated objects on display here – such as gilded hand-mirrors and lacquer boxes – allude to the life of elegance and indulgence led by courtesans a thousand years ago. (Honkan Room 3-2)

Samurai Armour & Swords

Glistening swords, finely stitched armour and imposing helmets bring the samurai – those iconic warriors of Japan's medieval age – to life. (Honkan Rooms 5 & 6)

Ukiyo-e & Kimono

Lavish silken kimono are displayed alongside lushly coloured *ukiyo-e* (wood-block prints). Both are icons of the Edo-era (1603–1868) *ukiyo* (literally 'the floating world') – the world of fleeting beauty and pleasure inhabited by the kabuki actors, courtesans and moneyed merchants who set the fashions of the day. (Honkan Room 10)

Gallery of Hōryū-ji Treasures

The Gallery of Hōryū-ji Treasures displays masks, scrolls and gilt Buddhas from the temple Hōryū-ji (founded in 607). It's a separate structure, a spare, elegant building by Taniguchi Yoshio, who also designed New York's Museum of Modern Art (MoMA).

☑ Top Tips

▶ It's open 9.30am–5pm Tuesday to Thursday year round, to 8pm Friday, to 6pm Saturday & Sunday (March to December).

▶ Admission costs for adult/student/child & senior are ¥620/¥410/free.

▶ Allow two hours to take in the highlights, a half-day to do the Honkan in depth or a whole day to take in everything.

▶ Be sure to pick up the brochure *Highlights of Japanese Art*, found in room 1-1 on the 2nd floor of the Honkan.

▶ Exhibits rotate to protect works and present seasonal displays, so there's no guarantee that a particular work will be on display.

✗ Take a Break

The charming teahouse Torindō (p130) is a five-minute walk northwest of the museum. The museum complex also has restaurants in the Gallery of Hōryū-ji Treasures and in the Tōyōkan.

Local Life
An Afternoon in Historic Yanaka

In a city where the sentiment 'new is better' goes almost unquestioned, Yanaka stands out for having a profound connection to the old. Having survived the Great Kantō Earthquake and the allied firebombing of WWII, Yanaka has a high concentration of vintage wooden structures and temples. The neighbourhood has long been popular with artists and many live and work here.

....

1 Stroll Yanaka Ginza
Yanaka Ginza is pure vintage mid-20th-century Tokyo, a cluster of street stalls that feels like a bustling village thoroughfare. Stop in **Yanaka Matsunoya** (谷中松屋; www.matsunoya. jp; 3-14-14 Nishi-Nippori, Arakawa-ku; ⊙11am-7pm Wed-Mon, from 10am Sat & Sun; ℝ JR Yamanote line to Nippori, west exit), which sells household goods handmade by local artisans.

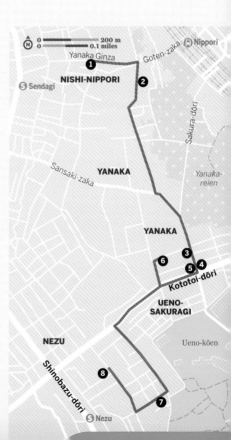

❷ Explore an Artist's Home

Sculptor Asakura Fumio (artist name Chōso; 1883–1964) designed this fanciful house and studio himself. It's now the **Asakura Chōso Museum** (朝倉彫塑館; www.taitocity.net/taito/asakura; 7-16-10 Yanaka, Taitō-ku; adult/student ¥400/150; ⏱9.30am-4.30pm Tue-Thu, Sat & Sun; 🚃JR Yamanote line to Nippori, north exit), with a number of the artist's signature realist works on display.

❸ See Art in a Bathhouse

For 200 years, this graceful structure with a sloping tile roof was a public bathhouse. In 1993 it became **SCAI the Bathhouse** (スカイザバスハウス; ☎3821-1144; www.scaithebathhouse. com; 6-1-23 Yanaka, Taitō-ku; admission free; ⏱noon-6pm Tue-Sat; Ⓢ Chiyoda line to Nezu, exit 1), a contemporary-art gallery, but retains plenty of original elements, including the wooden lockers and the vaulted ceiling.

❹ Visit a 100-Year-Old Shop

Shitamachi Museum Annex (下町風俗資料館; 2-10-6 Ueno-sakuragi, Taitō-ku; admission free; ⏱9.30am-4.30pm Tue-Sun; Ⓢ Chiyoda line to Nezu, exit 1) preserves an old liquor shop that operated from 1910 to 1986, complete with old sake barrels, weights, measures and posters.

❺ Hang Out at Kayaba Coffee

Across the street from the Shitamachi Museum Annex is local hang out **Kayaba Coffee** (カヤバ珈琲; http://kayaba-coffee.com; 6-1-29 Yanaka, Taitō-ku; drinks from ¥400; ⏱8am-11pm Mon-Sat, to 6pm Sun; Ⓢ Chiyoda line to Nezu, exit 1), which has been in business since the 1930s (the building itself dates to 1916) and still has many vintage fixtures.

❻ Peek Inside a Working Studio

A long-time Yanaka resident, Allan West paints gorgeous screens in the traditional Japanese style, making his paints from scratch just as local artists have done for centuries. Visitors are welcome to peek inside his **studio** (繪処アランウエスト; ☎3827-1907; www.allanwest.jp; 1-6-17 Yanaka, Taitō-ku; admission free; ⏱1-5pm, from 3pm Sun; Ⓢ Chiyoda line to Nezu, exit 1) when he's there.

❼ Bathe at Rokuryu Kōsen

Join the locals for a soak at **Rokuryu Kōsen** (六龍鉱泉; 3-4-20 Ikenohata, Taitō-ku; admission ¥460; ⏱3.30-11pm Tue-Sun; Ⓢ Chiyoda line to Nezu, exit 2), a public bathhouse since 1931. Ancient leaves work their way up the pipes here, giving the water an amber hue (and a mineral content said to be good for one's skin). Don't miss the fantastic traditional wall murals.

❽ Noodles at Kamachiku

Udon (thick wheat noodles) made fresh daily is the specialty at **Kamachiku** (釜竹; ☎5815-4675; http://kamachiku.com/top_en; 2-14-18 Nezu, Bunkyō-ku; noodles from ¥850, small dishes ¥350-850; ⏱11.30am-2pm Tue-Sun, 5-9pm Tue-Sat; Ⓢ Chiyoda line to Nezu, exit 1). This popular restaurant fills a beautifully restored brick warehouse from 1910. Expect to queue on weekends.

For reviews see

◉	Top Sights	p122
◎	Sights	p127
✕	Eating	p129
🍷	Drinking	p130
🛍	Shopping	p131

Nishi Nippori

ARAKAWA-KU

0 ⎯⎯⎯ 200 m
0 ⎯⎯⎯ 0.1 miles

NISHI-NIPPORI

Yanaka Ginza 16

Nippori

Ⓢ Sendagi

Ogubashi-dōri

Otakebashi-dōri

Sakura-dōri

🔒 19

Yanaka-reien 8

18

NEGISHI

YANAKA

Kototoi-dōri

14 ✕

BUNKYŌ-KU

Kototoi-dōri

UENO-SAKURAGI

17

Gallery of Hōryū-ji Treasures

Uguisudani

●Kanei-ji

Heiseikan

NEZU

Tokyo National University of Fine Arts & Music

Honkan

Tokyo National Museum ◉

TAITŌ-KU

Iriya

Ⓢ

12 ✕

Kuro-mon

Tōyōkan

Shuto Expwy No 1

Nezu Ⓢ

IKE-NO-HATA

Ueno Zoo 9

Ueno-kōen

National Science Museum

◎ 1

10 ◎

KITA-UENO

Ueno Tōshō-gū 2

UENO

Shinobazu-dōri

Kiyōmizu Kannon-dō

3

Keisei Ueno

HIGASHI-UENO

Inarichō Ⓢ

Yokoyama Taikan Memorial Hall

7

Bōto-ike

Benten-dō

Ⓢ Ueno

Asakusa-dōri

Shinobazu-ike

5 Shitamachi Museum

Tourist Information Centre 🅸

15

HONGŌ

Kyū Iwasaki-teien ◎ 6

13

4 Ameya-yokochō

HIGASHI-UENO

Yushima Ⓢ

11 ✕

Ueno-hirokōji Ⓢ

Nakamachi-dōri

Chūō-dōri

Ueno-Okachimachi

Okachimachi

Ⓢ

Naka-Okachimachi

Kasuga-dōri

Shin-Okachimachi Ⓢ

Ueno-Okachimachi

Sights

Ueno-kōen   PARK

1 ⊙ Map p126, C4

Sprawling Ueno-kōen has wooded pathways that wind past centuries-old temples and shrines – even a zoo. At the southern tip is a large pond, Shinobazu-ike, choked with lily pads. Stroll down the causeway to **Benten-dō** (弁天堂; Map p126; ☎3821-4638; 2-1 Ueno-kōen, Taitō-ku; admission free; ⊙9am-5pm; ®JR Yamanote line to Ueno, exit), a temple dedicated to Benzaiten (the water goddess). From here you can get a good look at the birds and botany that thrive in the park; you can also rent row boats (per hour ¥600). Navigating the park is easy, thanks to large maps in English. (上野公園; ⊙5am-11pm; ®JR Yamanote line to Ueno, Ueno-kōen & Shinobazu exits)

Ueno Tōshō-gū   SHINTO SHRINE

2 ⊙ Map p126, B4

Like its counterpart in Nikkō, this shrine inside Ueno-kōen was built in honour of Tokugawa Ieyasu, the warlord who unified Japan. Resplendent in gold leaf and ornate details, it dates from 1651 (though it recently underwent a touch-up). You can get a pretty-good look from outside the gate, if you want to skip the admission fee. (上野東照宮; www.uenotoshogu.com; 9-88 Ueno-kōen, Taitō-ku; admission ¥500; ⊙9.30am-4.30pm; ®JR Yamanote line to Ueno, Shinobazu exit)

Kiyōmizu Kannon-dō   BUDDHIST TEMPLE

3 ⊙ Map p126, C4

Ueno-kōen's Kiyōmizu Kannon-dō is one of Tokyo's oldest structures: established in 1631 and in its present position since 1698, it has survived every disaster that has come its way. It's a miniature of the famous Kiyomizu-dera in Kyoto and is a pilgrimage site for women hoping to conceive. (清水観音堂; 1-29 Ueno-kōen, Taitō-ku; ⊙9am-4pm; ®JR Yamanote line to Ueno, Shinobazu exit)

Ameya-yokochō   MARKET

4 ⊙ Map p126, C5

Step into this alley paralleling the JR Yamanote-line tracks, and ritzy, glitzy Tokyo feels like a distant memory. This open-air market got its start as a black market, post WWII, when American goods were sold here. Today, it's filled with vendors selling everything from fresh seafood and exotic cooking spices to jeans and sneakers. (アメヤ横町; 4 Ueno, Taitō-ku; ®JR Yamanote line to Ueno, Ueno-kōen exit)

Top Tip

Megurin Bus

The Tōzai Megurin bus (¥100) does a neat loop around Ueno and neighbouring Yanaka. Pick up a map at the **Tourist Information Center** (Map p126, C5; ⊙9.30am-6.30pm) at Keisei Ueno Station.

Understand
Ueno-kōen

- -

Established in 1873, Ueno-kōen is known as Japan's first public park (in the Western sense), but it's much older than that. Structures here date as far back as the 17th century. There's a Kiyōmizu Kannon-dō (p127), modelled after the landmark temple in Kyoto, and a Tōshō-gū (p127; Shintō shrine) similar to the shrine in Nikkō. **Shinobazu-ike** (不忍池; pond), where couples now paddle swan-shaped boats, was likened to the country's central Lake Biwa and Ueno-kōen was billed as a mini-Japan – a sort of prototypical Disney World. During the Edo period (1603-1868), when travel was heavily restricted, Tokyoites could 'see' the country without having to leave home. The park's reputation as the most famous *hanami* (cherry-blossom viewing) spot in the city dates to this era.

Shitamachi Museum   MUSEUM

 5 Map p126, C5

This museum re-creates life in the plebeian quarters of Tokyo during the Meiji and Taishō periods (1868–1926), before the city was twice destroyed by the Great Kanto Earthquake (1923) and WWII. There are old tenement houses and shops that you can enter. (下町風俗資料館; ☑3823-7451; www.taitocity.net/taito/shitamachi; 2-1 Ueno-kōen, Taitō-ku; adult/child ¥300/100; ◷9.30am-4.30pm Tue-Sun; ▣JR Yamanote line to Ueno, Shinobazu exit)

Kyū Iwasaki-teien   HISTORIC BUILDING

 6 Map p126, B5

This grand residence was once the villa of Hisaya Iwasaki, son of the founder of Mitsubishi, and is now a fascinating example of how the cultural elite of the early Meiji period tried to straddle east and west. Built in 1896, it has been open to the public since 2001. (旧岩崎邸庭園; ☑3823-8340; http://teien.tokyo-park.or.jp/en/kyu-iwasaki/index.html; 1-3-45 Ike-no-hata, Taitō-ku; adult/child ¥400/free; ◷9am-5pm; ⑤Chiyoda line to Yushima, exit 1)

Yokoyama Taikan Memorial Hall   MUSEUM

7 Map p126, B4

Early-20th-century artist Yokoyama Taikan was one of the masters of modern *nihonga* (Japanese-style painting). Inside his former residence, a traditional Japanese structure with a garden, are changing displays of his works and those of his contemporaries. The museum closes for several weeks in June, August and December. (横山大観記念館; http://members2.jcom.home.ne.jp/taikan/index.htm; 1-4-24 Ike-no-hata, Taitō-ku; adult/child ¥550/200; ◷10am-4pm Thu-Sun; ⑤Chiyoda line to Yushima, exit 1)

Yanaka-reien
CEMETERY

8 ◎ Map p126, B2

One of Tokyo's largest graveyards, Yanaka-reien is the final resting place of more than 7000 souls, many of whom were quite well known in their day. It's also where you'll find the tomb of Yoshinobu Tokugawa (徳川慶喜の墓), the last shōgun. (谷中霊園; 7-5-24 Yanaka, Taitō-ku; R JR Yamanote line to Nippori, west exit)

Ueno Zoo
ZOO

9 ◎ Map p126, B4

Japan's oldest zoo is home to animals from around the globe, but the biggest attractions are two giant pandas that arrived from China in 2011 – Rī Rī and Shin Shin. There's also a whole area devoted to lemurs, which makes sense given Tokyoites' love of all things cute. (上野動物園; Ueno Dōbutsu-en; www.tokyo-zoo.net; 9-83 Ueno-kōen, Taitō-ku; adult/child ¥600/free; ⏱9.30am-5pm Tue-Sun; R JR Yamanote line to Ueno, Ueno-kōen exit)

National Science Museum
MUSEUM

10 ◎ Map p126, C4

The Japan Gallery here showcases the rich and varied wildlife of the Japanese archipelago, from the bears of Hokkaidō to the giant beetles of Okinawa. Elsewhere in the museum: a rocket launcher, a giant squid, an Edo-era mummy, and a digital seismograph that charts earthquakes in real time. There's English signage throughout, plus an English-language audio guide (¥300). (国立科学博物館, Kokuritsu Kagaku Hakubutsukan; www.kahaku.go.jp; 7-20 Ueno-kōen, Taitō-ku; adult/child ¥600/free; ⏱9am-5pm Tue-Thu, Sat & Sun, to 8pm Fri; R JR Yamanote line to Ueno, Ueno-kōen exit)

Eating

Shinsuke
IZAKAYA $$

11 Map p126, B5

In business since 1925, Shinsuke is pretty much the platonic ideal of an *izakaya*: long cedar counter, 'master' in *happi* (traditional short coat) and *hachimaki* (traditional headband), and smooth-as-silk *dai-ginjo* (premium-grade sake). The only part that seems out of place is the friendly staff who go out of their way to explain the dishes in English. (シンスケ; ☎3832-0469; 3-31-5 Yushima, Bunkyō-ku; ⏱5-9.30pm Mon-Fri, to 9pm Sat; S Chiyoda line to Yushima, exit 3)

Hantei
TRADITIONAL JAPANESE $$

12 Map p126, A3

Housed in a beautifully maintained, century-old traditional wooden building, Hantei is a local landmark. Delectable skewers of seasonal *kushi-age* (fried meat, fish and vegetables) are served with small, refreshing side dishes. Lunch courses include eight sticks and dinner courses start with six, after which you'll continue to receive additional rounds (¥210 per skewer) until you say stop. (はん亭; ☎3828-1440; www.hantei.co.jp/nedu.html;

2-12-15 Nezu, Bunkyō-ku; lunch/dinner courses from ¥3150/2835; ⏱noon-3pm & 5-10pm Tue-Sun; §Chiyoda line to Nezu, exit 2)

Izu-ei Honten
UNAGI $$

13 🍴 Map p126, C5

Izu-ei's twin delights are its delicious *unagi* (eel) and its elegant, traditional atmosphere, with tatami seating (there's chairs, too) and waitresses in kimonos. (伊豆栄本店; www.izuei.co.jp; 2-12-22 Ueno, Taitō-ku; set meals ¥2160-4860; ⏱11am-9.30pm; ®JR Yamanote line to Ueno, Hirokōji exit)

Sasa-no-Yuki
TOFU $$

14 🍴 Map p126, C2

Sasa-no-Yuki opened its doors in the Edo period, and continues to serve its signature dishes, with tofu made fresh every morning with water from the shop's own well. Some treats to

---

 Local Life

Snack Time

Locals love **Nezu no Taiyaki** (根津のたいやき; Map p126, A3; 1-23-9-104 Nezu, Bunkyō-ku; taiyaki ¥170; ⏱10.30am until sold out, closed irregularly; 🍴; §Chiyoda line to Nezu, exit 1). This street stall, in business for half a century, specialises in just one thing: *taiyaki*, hot, sweet bean jam buns shaped like *tai* (sea bream) – a fish considered to be lucky. Come early before they sell out (always by 2pm, and sometimes by noon).

---

expect: *ankake-dofu* (tofu in a thick, sweet sauce) and *goma-dofu* (sesame tofu). The best seats overlook a tiny garden with a koi pond. (笹乃雪; 📞3873-1145; 2-15-10 Negishi, Taitō-ku; dishes ¥400-700, lunch/dinner courses from ¥2200/5000; ⏱11.30am-8pm Tue-Sun; 🍴; ®JR Yamanote line to Uguisudani, north exit)

Yabu Soba
SOBA $

15 🍴 Map p126, C5

This busy, famous place rustles up top-class *soba* (buckwheat noodles). There's a picture menu to help you choose. Look for the black-granite sign in front that says in English 'Since 1892'. (上野やぶそば; 📞3831-4728; 6-9-16 Ueno, Taitō-ku; ⏱11.30am-8.30pm Thu-Tue; ®JR Yamanote line to Ueno, Hirokōji exit)

Nagomi
YAKITORI $$

16 🍴 Map p126, B2

On Yanaka Ginza, Nagomi deals in juicy skewers of *ji-dori* (free-range chicken). There are plenty of grilled veggie options, too. Wash it all down with a bowl of chicken soup *rāmen*. Look for the sake bottles in the window. (和味; 📞3821-5972; 3-11-11 Yanaka, Taitō-ku; skewers from ¥180; ⏱5pm-midnight; ®JR Yamanote line to Nippori, north exit; 🍴)

Drinking

Torindō
TEAHOUSE

17 ☕ Map p126, B3

Sample a cup of paint-thick *matcha* (powdered green tea) at this tiny

Japanese macaques at Ueno Zoo (p129)

teahouse on the edge of Ueno-kōen. Tradition dictates that the bitter tea be paired with something sweet, so choose from the artful desserts in the glass counter, then pull up a stool at the communal table. It's a white building with persimmon-coloured door curtains. (桃林堂; 1-5-7 Ueno-Sakuragi, Taitō-ku; tea sets ¥810; ⊙9am-5pm; ⑤Chiyoda line to Nezu, exit 1)

Bousingot

18 🚇 Map p126, A2

BAR

It's fitting that Yanaka, which refuses to trash the past, would have a bar that doubles as a used bookshop. Sure, the books are in Japanese but you can still enjoy soaking up the atmosphere with some resident book lovers. (ブーザンゴ; ☑3823-5501; www.bousingot. com; 2-33-2 Sendagi, Bunkyō-ku; drinks from ¥450; ⊙6-11pm Wed-Mon; ⑤Chiyoda line to Sendagi, exit 1)

Shopping

Isetatsu

CRAFTS

19 🔒 Map p126, A2

Dating back to 1864, this venerable stationery shop specialises in *chiyogami*: gorgeous, colourful paper made using woodblocks. (いせ辰; ☑3823-1453; 2-18-9 Yanaka, Taitō-ku; ⊙10am-6pm; ⑤Chiyoda line to Sendagi, exit 1)

Explore

Asakusa

Asakusa (ah-saku-sah) is home to Tokyo's oldest attraction, the centuries-old temple Sensō-ji. Just across the river is the city's newest: the 634m-tall Tokyo Sky Tree. The neighbourhoods surrounding these sights are known as *shitamachi* (the low city), where the spirit of old Edo (Tokyo under the shogun) proudly lives on in an atmospheric web of alleys, artisan shops and mum-and-dad restaurants.

The Sights in a Day

☀ Begin your journey through this historic district at Asakusa Station, following the signs to Kaminarimon (Thunder Gate). Just outside, look across the river to the architectural landmark, **Super Dry Hall** (p137). Then head down the Nakamise-dōri shopping arcade leading to the temple **Sensō-ji** (p134). Spend an hour exploring the temple and neighbouring **Asakusa-jinja** (p137), then stop for a lunch of tempura at **Daikokuya** (p139).

☀ In the afternoon stroll around Asakusa's atmospheric side streets, stopping at **Chingo-dō** (p137), the **Traditional Crafts Museum** (p139), the **Taiko Drum Museum** (p139) and some of the traditional crafts shops. Stop for a coffee at **Ef** (p141), or revive yourself in the classic Japanese way – with a soak in the hot-spring tubs at neighbourhood bathhouse **Jakotsu-yu** (p137).

☾ Have dinner at historic **Komagata Dojō** (p139), or go for filling *okonomiyaki* (savoury pancake) at **Sometarō** (p140). Then hop on the Tōbu Sky Tree line (or take a taxi) for **Tokyo Sky Tree** (p137), across the river. Take the lift from the 4th floor up to the observatories at 350m for dazzling night views over the city.

Top Sights
Sensō-ji (p134)

♥ Best of Tokyo
Architecture
Super Dry Hall (p137)

Temples & Shrines
Asakusa-jinja (p137)

Eating
Komagata Dojō (p139)

Sentō & Onsen
Jakotsu-yu (p137)

Shopping
Bengara (p142)

Traditional Theatre & Dance
Asakusa Engei Hall (p142)

Getting There

🚃 **Train** The Tōbu Sky Tree line leaves from Tōbu Asakusa Station for Tokyo Sky Tree Station.

🅂 **Subway** Ginza line stops at Asakusa and Tawaramachi. The Asakusa line also stops at Asakusa at a separate station south of the Ginza line. Hanzōmon line stops at Oshiage for Tokyo Sky Tree.

⚓ **Ferry** Azuma-bashi is the starting point for Tokyo Cruise water buses heading to Hama-rikyū Onshi-teien.

Top Sights
Sensō-ji

Founded more than 1000 years before Tokyo got its start, Sensō-ji is the capital's oldest temple and the spiritual home of its ancestors. According to legend, in AD 628 two fishermen brothers pulled a golden image of Kannon (the Buddhist Goddess of Mercy) out of the nearby Sumida-gawa. The temple was built to enshrine it. Today Sensō-ji stands out for its old-world atmosphere – offering a glimpse of a bygone Japan that can be difficult to find in contemporary Tokyo.

浅草寺

Map p136, B2

☏ 3842-0181

www.senso-ji.jp

2-3-1 Asakusa, Taitō-ku

🕐 24hr

Ⓢ Ginza line to Asakusa, exit 1

Sensō-ji

Don't Miss

Kaminari-mon

The temple precinct begins at the majestic Kaminari-mon, which houses a pair of ferocious protective deities: Fūjin, the god of wind, on the right; and Raijin, the god of thunder, on the left.

Nakamise-dōri

Straight on through the gate is the bustling shopping street known as Nakamise-dōri. There are stalls selling all sorts of things – from souvenirs to genuine Edo-style crafts to sweet *age-manjū* (deep-fried buns stuffed with *anko* – bean paste).

Five-Storey Pagoda

This 53m-high, five-storey pagoda is a 1973 reconstruction of the one built by Tokugawa Iemitsu in the 17th century. It's the second-highest pagoda in Japan.

Main Hall

In front of the grand main hall is a large incense cauldron. The smoke is said to bestow health and you'll see people rubbing it into their bodies through their clothes. The ancient image of Kannon is not on public display (and admittedly may not exist at all), but this doesn't stop a steady stream of worshippers from paying their respects.

Getting Your Fortune

Before the main hall, plunk down ¥100 for an *omikuji* (fortune). Shake the silver canister and extract a stick, noting its number (in kanji). Find the matching drawer and withdraw a paper fortune (there's English on the back). If you get a bad one just tie the paper on the nearby rack, ask the gods for better luck and try again.

TOM BONAVENTURE/GETTY IMAGES ©

☑ Top Tips

▶ Admission is free

▶ The main hall and its gates are illuminated every day from sunset until 11pm. The minutes just before the sun sinks make for some of the best pictures of this photogenic sanctuary.

▶ Consider the crowds part of the experience, as there doesn't seem to be a time of day when Sensō-ji isn't packed.

✗ Take a Break

There are numerous snack vendors, like Chōchin Monaka (p140) lining Nakamise-dōri.

Just off of Nakamise-dōri, Daikokuya (p139) serves delicious tempura in an unpretentious setting that is typical of Asakusa.

0 200 m
0 0.1 miles

IMADO

ASAKUSA

TAITŌ-KU

NISHI-ASAKUSA

HANAKAWADO

KAMINARI-MON

ASAKUSA

KOMAGATA

KURAME

KUEAME

KOTOBUKI

HIGASHI-MUKŌJIMA

MUKŌJIMA

HIGASHI-KOMAGATA

NARIHIRA

OSHIAGE

Sumida-kōen

Sumida-kōen

Kototoi-dōri

Yoshino-dōri

Mitsume-dōri

Kototoi-dōri

Kokusai-dōri

Kappabashi Hon-dōri

Kappabashi-dōri

Tawaramachi

Asakusa-dōri

Kaminari-mon-dōri

Dembōin-dōri

Kasuga-dōri

Komagata-bashi

Shin-Nakamise-dōri

Nakamise-dōri

Umamichi-dōri

Edo-dōri

Hisago-dōri

Hoppy-dōri

Chingo-dō

Sensō-ji

Five-Storey Pagoda

Traditional Crafts Museum

Asakusa-jinja

Tōbu Asakusa

Asakusa

Shuto Expwy No 6

Sumida River (Sumida-gawa)

Kototoi-bashi

Tokyo Sky Tree Station

Tokyo Sky Tree

Oshiage

Honjo-Azumabashi

Super Dry Hall

Tokyo Cruise Asakusa Pier

Asakusa Culture Tourist Information Center

Tsukuba Express Asakusa

Jakotsu-yu

Taiko Drum Museum

Mokurikan

1 2 3 4 5 6 7 8 9 10 11 12 13 15 16 17 18 19 20 21 22 23 24 25

Sights

Asakusa-jinja
SHINTO SHRINE

1 Map p136, B2

Asakusa-jinja was built in honour of the brothers who discovered the Kannon statue that inspired the construction of Sensō-ji. The current building, painted a deep shade of red, dates to 1649 and is a rare example of early-Edo architecture. It's also the epicentre of one of Tokyo's most important festivals, May's Sanja Matsuri. (浅草神社; ☎3844-1575; www.asakusajinja.jp/english; 2-3-1 Asakusa, Taitō-ku; ⏰9am-4.30pm; ⑤Ginza line to Asakusa, exit 1)

Tokyo Sky Tree
TOWER

2 Map p136, E3

Tokyo Sky Tree opened in May 2012 as the world's tallest 'free-standing tower' at 634m. Its silvery exterior of steel mesh morphs from a triangle at the base to a circle at 300m. There are two observation decks, at 350m and 450m. You can see more stuff during daylight hours – at peak visibility you can see up to 100km away, all the way to Mt Fuji – but it is at night that Tokyo appears truly beautiful. (東京スカイツリー; www.tokyo-skytree.jp; 1-1-2 Oshiage, Sumida-ku; admission 350m/450m observation decks ¥2060/3090; ⏰8am-10pm; ⑤Hanzōmon line to Oshiage, Sky Tree exit)

Super Dry Hall
ARCHITECTURE

3 Map p136, C3

Designed by Philippe Starck and completed in 1989, the Asahi Beer headquarters, with its telltale golden plume, is a Tokyo landmark. The golden bit – which weighs more than 300 tonnes – is open to interpretation: Asahi likes to think it is the foam to the building's beer mug. Locals call it the 'golden turd'. (フラムドール; Flamme d'Or; 1-23-1 Azuma-bashi, Sumida-ku; ⑤Ginza line to Asakusa, exit 4)

Chingo-dō
BUDDHIST TEMPLE

4 Map p136, B2

This small, peaceful temple is actually part of Sensō-ji but has a separate entrance on Dembo-in-dōri. It pays tribute to the *tanuki* (racoon-like folkloric characters), who figure in Japanese myth as mystical shape-shifters and merry pranksters. They are also said to protect against fire and theft, which is why you'll often see *tanuki* figurines in front of restaurants. (鎮護堂; 2-3-1 Asakusa, Taitō-ku; ⏰6am-5pm; ⑤Ginza line to Asakusa, exit 1)

Jakotsu-yu
SENTO

5 Map p136, B3

Unlike most *sentō* (public baths), the tubs here are filled with pure hot-

---

Top Tip

Tokyo Sky Tree View

Head to the 8th floor of the Asakusa Culture Tourist Information Center for perfect (and free!) views of Tokyo Sky Tree.

Understand
Old Edo & Shitamachi

Before Tokyo there was Edo – literally 'Gate of the River' – named for its location at the mouth of the Sumida-gawa. This small farming village rose from obscurity in 1603 when Tokugawa Ieyasu established his shōgunate (military government) here. The new capital quickly transformed into a bustling city and by the late 18th century was the largest city in the world with a population of one million.

Life in Old Edo
Under Tokugawa rule, society was rigidly hierarchical. At the top were the *daimyō* (feudal lords) and their samurai. Then came the peasants – the farmers and fishermen – and at the bottom were the *chōnin*, the townspeople, including merchants and artisans. The layout of Edo, too, was divided: on the elevated plain to the west of the castle was the *yamanote* (literally 'mountain's hand'), where the feudal elite built its estates. In the east, along the banks of the Sumida-gawa, the *chōnin* lived elbow to elbow in wooden tenement houses in *shitamachi* (the low-lying parts of Edo).

Wealth, however, didn't follow such neat lines; in reality, some *chōnin* grew fabulously wealthy and enjoyed a lifestyle that thumbed its nose at the austerity prescribed by the ruling class. It was they who patronised the kabuki theatre, sumo tournaments and the pleasure district of Yoshiwara, to the north of Asakusa.

Shitamachi Today
While official class distinctions were laid to rest along with feudalism in the 19th century, the old city patterns remain. Former *shitamachi* districts to the east, such as Asakusa, are still a tangle of alleys and tightly packed quarters, with more traditional architecture, old-school artisans and small businesses.

Even today, the word *shitamachi* is used to describe such neighbourhoods that come closest to approximating the spirit of old Edo. Those who've lived in such districts for generations can call themselves *Edokko*, or children of Edo. And even some who don't qualify are finding themselves increasingly drawn to such neighbourhoods, which offer the human connections and warmth lacking in newer parts of the city.

spring water, the colour of weak tea. Another treat is the lovely, lantern-lit, rock-framed *rotemburo* (outdoor bath). Jakotsu-yu is a welcoming place; it has English signage and doesn't have a policy against tattoos. It's an extra ¥200 for the sauna; ¥140 for a small towel. (蛇骨湯; 3841-8645; www.jakotsuyu.co.jp; 1-11-11 Asakusa, Taitō-ku; admission ¥460; ⏰1pm-midnight Wed-Mon; Ⓢ Ginza line to Tawaramachi, exit 3)

Mokuhankan PRINTMAKING

6 ◎ Map p136, B2

Try your hand at making *ukiyo-e* (woodblock prints) at this studio run by expat David Bull. Hour-long 'print parties' take place daily; sign up online. There's a shop here too, where you can see Bull and Jed Henry's humorous Ukiyo-e Heroes series – prints featuring video-game characters in traditional settings. (木版館; ☏070-5011-1418; http://mokuhankan.com/parties; 2nd fl, 1-41-8 Asakusa, Taitō-ku; per person ¥2000; ⏰10am-5.30pm; Ⓡ Tsukuba Express to Asakusa, exit 5)

Taiko Drum Museum MUSEUM

7 ◎ Map p136, A3

There are hundreds of drums from around the world here, including several traditional Japanese *taiko*. The best part is that you can actually play most of them (those marked with a music note). (太鼓館; Taiko-kan; www.miyamoto-unosuke.co.jp/taikokan; 4th fl, 2-1-1 Nishi-Asakusa, Taitō-ku; adult/child ¥500/150; ⏰10am-5pm Wed-Sun; Ⓢ Ginza line to Tawaramachi, exit 3)

Traditional Crafts Museum MUSEUM

8 ◎ Map p136, B1

Asakusa has a long artisan tradition and changing exhibitions of local crafts, such as *Edo-kiriko* (cut glass), are on display here. Demonstrations are held on Saturdays and Sundays (between 11am and 5pm). (江戸下町伝統工芸館, Edo Shitamachi Dentō Kōgeikan; www.city.taito. lg.jp/index/kurashi/shigoto/jibasangyo/kogeikan; 2-22-13 Asakusa, Taitō-ku; admission free; ⏰10am-8pm; Ⓢ Ginza line to Asakusa, exit 1)

Eating

Komagata Dojō TRADITIONAL JAPANESE $

9 ✗ Map p136, B4

Since 1801, Komagata Dojō has been stewing *dojō* (Japanese loach, which looks a bit like a miniature eel). *Dojō-nabe* (loach hotpot), served here on individual *hibachi* (charcoal stoves), was a common dish in the days of Edo, but few restaurants serve it today. The open seating around wide wooden planks heightens the traditional flavour. There are lanterns out front. (駒形どぜう; ☏3842-4001; 1-7-12 Komagata, Taitō-ku; mains from ¥1550; ⏰11am-9pm; Ⓢ Ginza line to Asakusa, exits A2 & A4)

Daikokuya TEMPURA $

10 ✗ Map p136, B2

Near Nakamise-dōri, this is the place to get old-fashioned tempura fried in pure sesame oil, an Asakusa speciality. It's in a white building with a tile roof. If there's a queue (and there often is), you can try your luck at the annexe one block over. (大黒家; www.tempura.co.jp/english/index.html; 1-38-10 Asakusa, Taitō-ku; meals ¥1550-2100; ⏰11am-8.30pm Mon-Fri, to 9pm Sat; Ⓢ Ginza line to Asakusa, exit 1)

Sometarō OKONOMIYAKI $

 11 Map p136, A3

Sometarō is a fun and funky place to try *okonomiyaki* (savoury Japanese-style pancakes filled with meat, seafood and vegetables that you cook yourself). This historic, vine-covered house is a friendly spot where the menu includes a how-to guide for even the most culinarily challenged. (染太郎; 2-2-2 Nishi-Asakusa, Taitō-ku; mains ¥390-880; ⏰noon-10pm; Ⓢ Ginza line to Tawaramachi, exit 3)

Irokawa UNAGI $$

 12 Map p136, B3

This tiny restaurant has a real old Edo flavour and is one of the best, unpretentious *unagi* (eel) restaurants in town. The menu is simple: a 'small' gets you two slices of charcoal-grilled eel over rice, a 'large' gets you three. The chef grills everything right behind the counter. Look for the light-green building with plants out front. (色川; ☎3844-1187; 2-6-11 Kaminari-mon, Taitō-ku; sets from ¥2500; ⏰11.30am-1.30pm & 5-8.30pm Mon-Sat; Ⓢ Ginza line to Asakusa, exit 2)

Asakusa Imahan SUKIYAKI $$$

 13 Map p136, A2

Swing by this famous beef restaurant, in business since 1895. Choose between courses of *sukiyaki* (sautéed beef dipped in raw egg) and *shabu-shabu* (beef blanched in broth); prices rise according to the grade of meat. For diners on a budget, Imahan sells a limited number of cheaper lunch sets (from ¥1500). (浅草今半; ☎3841-1114; www.asakusaimahan.co.jp/index.html; 3-1-1 Nishi-Asakusa, Taitō-ku; lunch/dinner courses from ¥3780/7130; ⏰11.30am-9.30pm; Ⓢ Ginza line to Tawaramachi, exit 3)

Rokurinsha RĀMEN $

14 Map p136, E3

Rokurinsha's specialty is *tsukemen – rāmen* noodles served on the side with a bowl of concentrated soup for dipping. The noodles here are thick and perfectly al dente and the soup is a rich *tonkotsu* (pork bone) base. It's an addictive combination that draws lines to this outpost in Tokyo Sky Tree Town. (六厘舎; www.rokurinsha.com; 6th fl, Solamachi, 1-1-2 Oshiage, Sumida-ku; rāmen from ¥850; ⏰10.30am-11pm; Ⓢ Hanzōmon line to Oshiage, exit B3)

Chōchin Monaka SWEETS $

 15 Map p136, B2

Traditionally, *monaka* are wafers filled with sweet bean jam. This stand on Nakamise-dōri fills them with ice cream – in flavours such as *matcha* (powdered green tea) and *kuro-goma* (black sesame). (ちょうちんもなか; 2-3-1 Asakusa,

Plastic food for sale at Kappabashi-dōri (p143)

Taitō-ku; ice creams ¥280; ⏰10am-5.30pm; Ⓢ Ginza line to Asakusa, exit 1)

Drinking

Kamiya Bar
BAR

16 Ⓟ Map p136, B3

One of Tokyo's oldest Western-style bars, Kamiya opened in 1880 and is still hugely popular – though probably more so today for its enormous, cheap draught beer (¥1020 for a litre). It's real speciality, however, is Denki Bran, a herbal liquor that's been produced in-house for over a century. Order at the counter, then give your tickets to the server. (神谷バー; ☎3841-5400; www.kamiya-bar.com; 1-1-1 Asakusa, Taitō-ku;

⏰11.30am-10pm Wed-Mon; Ⓢ Ginza line to Asakusa, exit 3)

'Cuzn Homeground
BAR

17 Ⓟ Map p136, B2

Run by a wild gang of local hippies, 'Cuzn is the kind of bar where anything can happen: a barbecue, a jam session or all-night karaoke, for example. (http://homeground.jpn.com; 2-17-9 Asakusa, Taitō-ku; beer ¥800; ⏰11am-6am; 📶; Ⓢ Ginza line to Tawaramachi, exit 3)

Ef
CAFE

18 Ⓟ Map p136, B3

Set in a 19th-century wooden warehouse that survived the 1923 earthquake and WWII, this wonderfully cosy space serves coffee, tea and, after 6pm, cocktails and beer. Check out the gallery in the back. (エフ; ☎3841-0442; www.gallery-ef.com; 2-19-18 Kaminari-mon, Taitō-ku; coffee ¥550; ⏰11am-midnight Mon, Wed, Thu & Sat, to 2am Fri, to 10pm Sun; ⓈGinza line to Asakusa, exit 2)

Asahi Sky Room
BAR

19 Map p136, C3

Spend the day at the religious sites and end at the Asahi altar, on the 22nd floor of the golden-tinged Asahi Super Dry Building. The venue itself isn't noteworthy, but the views over the Sumida-gawa are spectacular, especially at sunset. (アサヒスカイルーム; ☎5608-5277; 22nd fl, Asahi Super Dry Bldg, 1-23-1 Azuma-bashi, Sumida-ku; beer ¥720; ⏰10am-9pm; ⓈGinza line to Asakusa, exit 4)

Entertainment

Asakusa Engei Hall
COMEDY

20 ⭐ Map p136, B2

Asakusa was once full of theatres like this one, where traditional *rakugo* (comedic monologue) and other forms of comedy are performed along with jugglers, magicians and the like. It's all in Japanese, but the linguistic confusion is mitigated by lively facial expressions and props, which help translate comic takes on universal human experiences. (浅草演芸ホール; ☎3841-6545; www.asakusaengei.com; 1-43-12 Asakusa, Taitō-ku; adult/student ¥2800/2300; ⏰shows 11.40am-4.30pm & 4.40-9pm; ⓈGinza line to Tawaramachi, exit 3)

Shopping

Bengara
CRAFTS

21 🔒 Map p136, B3

By now you're familiar with *noren*, the curtains that hang in front of shop doors. This store sells beautiful ones, made of linen and coloured with natural dyes (like indigo or persimmon) or decorated with ink-brush paintings. There are smaller items too, such as pouches and book covers, made of traditional textiles. (べんがら; www.bengara.com; 1-35-6 Asakusa, Taitō-ku; ⏰10am-6pm Mon-Fri, to 7pm Sat & Sun, closed 3rd Thu of month; ⓈGinza line to Asakusa, exit 1)

Tokyo Hotarudo
VINTAGE

This curio shop (see 6 Map p136, B2) is run by an eccentric young man who prefers to dress as if the 20th century hasn't come and gone already. If you think that sounds marvellous, then you'll want to check out his collection of vintage dresses and bags, antique lamps, watches, and objets d'art. (東京蛍堂; http://tokyohotarudo.com; 1-41-8 Asakusa, Taitō-ku; ⏰11am-8pm Wed-Sun; 🚈Tsukuba Express to Asakusa, exit 5)

Fujiya
CRAFTS

22 🔒 Map p136, B2

Fujiya specialises in *tenugui*: dyed cloths of thin cotton that can be used as tea towels, kerchiefs, gift wrap (the list goes on; they're surprisingly

Understand
Traditional Festivals

Tokyo's shrines host riotous *matsuri* (festivals) that seem to turn back the clock a few centuries. Men don *happi* (short-sleeve coats) and *fundoshi* (the traditional loincloths worn by sumo wrestlers) to carry *mikoshi* (portable shrines) through the streets, chanting as they push through the crowds. These celebrations have their roots in Shintō tradition, but they also serve to renew age-old community bonds. Asakusa's **Sanja Matsuri**, held the third weekend of May, is Tokyo's biggest, drawing some 1.5 million spectators annually; however, there are festivals throughout the year. Check for listings on **Go Tokyo** (www.gotokyo.org/en/index.html).

versatile). Here they come in traditional designs and humorous modern ones. (ふじ屋; 2-2-15 Asakusa, Taitō-ku; ⏰10.30am-6.30pm Fri-Wed; **S** Ginza line to Asakusa, exit 1)

Yonoya Kushiho
ACCESSORIES

23 🔒 Map p136, B2

Even in a neighbourhood where old is not out of place, Yonoya Kushiho stands out: this little shop has been selling handmade boxwood combs since 1717. Yonoya also sells old-fashioned hair ornaments (worn with the elaborate up-dos of courtesans in the past) and modern trinkets. (よのや櫛舗; 1-37-10 Asakusa, Taitō-ku; ⏰10.30am-6pm Thu-Tue; **S** Ginza line to Asakusa, exit 1)

Kappabashi-dōri
HOMEWARES

24 🔒 Map p136, A2

This street is most famous for its shops selling plastic food models,

but Kappabashi-dōri supplies many a Tokyo restaurant in bulk, selling matching sets of chopsticks, uniforms, woven bamboo tempura trays and tiny ceramic *shōyu* (soy sauce) dishes. This makes it the perfect street for stocking up if you're setting up an apartment or seeking small, useful souvenirs. (合羽橋通り; **S** Ginza Line to Tawaramachi, exit 3)

Solamachi
MALL

25 🔒 Map p136, E3

It's not all cheesy Sky Tree swag here at this mall under the tower (though you can get 634m-long rolls of Sky Tree toilet paper). Shops on the 4th floor offer a better-than-usual selection of Japanese-y souvenirs, including pretty trinkets made from kimono fabric and quirky fashion items. (ソラマチ; 1-1-2 Oshiage, Sumida-ku; ⏰10am-9pm; **S** Hanzōmon line to Oshiage, exit B3)

Top Sights
Ōedo Onsen Monogatari

Getting There

🚋 **Train** Take the Yurikamome line from Shiodome to Telecom Centre, south exit.

🚋 **Train** Take the Rinkai line from JR Ōsaki Station to Tokyo Teleport and transfer to the free shuttle bus.

Ōedo Onsen Monogatari proves that Tokyo really does have it all, even a natural hot spring. The water is pumped from a spring 1400m below Tokyo Bay. But Ōedo Onsen Monogatari is not solely about bathing. Billed as an 'onsen theme park' (a fantastically Japanese concept), it's done up to resemble a Disneyland-style version of an Edo-era town, with games and food stalls. Touristy, yes, but for visitors making their first foray into Japanese-style communal bathing, the light and kitschy atmosphere makes the actual bathing part that much less intimidating.

Ornamental foot bath at Ōedo Onsen Monogatari

Don't Miss

The Bathing Pools

Ōedo Onsen Monogatari has both indoor and outdoor tubs (called *rotemburo*) separated by gender. Part of the fun is hopping from bath to bath trying out the different temperatures and styles. There are jet baths, pools of natural rock and, on the ladies' side, personal bucket-shaped baths made of cedar. The water, rich in sodium chloride, is said to be good for aches and pains.

Wearing a Yukata

The first thing you'll do when you arrive is change into a *yukata*, a light, cotton kimono. You'll have your pick from a variety of colours; rental is included in the admission price. It's worn with the left side over the right, tied at the waist for women and at the hips for men. You can wear this around the communal areas too.

The Garden & Foot Bath

Outside is a Japanese-style garden with a 50m-long *ashi-yu* (foot bath) snaking through the centre. The ankle-deep water keeps your feet warm no matter how chilly the air. On the bottom are stones designed to stimulate the pressure points on the soles of the feet.

The Town

At the centre of the complex you'll find carnival-style games and food vendors, intended to re-create the feel of an old-time street festival – an atmosphere enhanced by the fact that everyone is in *yukata*. This is your chance to try your luck slinging *shuriken* (ninja throwing stars). The garden and town areas are communal, so mixed parties can hang out together.

大江戸温泉物語

www.ooedoonsen.jp

2-6-3 Aomi, Kōtō-ku

adult/child from ¥1980/900, after 6pm from ¥1480/900

⏱11am-9am, last entry 7am

☑ Top Tips

▶ Visit on a weekday afternoon, when it is less likely to be crowded.

▶ Visitors with tattoos will be denied admission.

✕ Take a Break

Take the Rinkai Line one stop to **TY Harbor Brewing** (☎5479-4555; www.tyharborbrewing.co.jp; 2-1-3 Higashi-Shinagawa, Shinagawa-ku; lunch sets ¥1200-1700; dinner mains from ¥1700; ⏱11.30am-2pm & 5.30-10pm; Ⓢ Rinkai line to Tennōzu Isle, exit B), a waterfront restaurant with an on-site brewery in an old warehouse.

There are also plenty of eating options within Ōedo Onsen Monogatari.

Top Sights
Mt Fuji

Getting There

Mt Fuji is 110km west of Tokyo.

🚌 **Keiō Dentetsu buses** (www.highwaybus. com; ¥1750, 1¾ hours; reservations necessary) depart from the Shinjuku Highway Terminal for Kawaguchi-ko.

Catching a glimpse of Mt Fuji (Fuji-san; 3776m), Japan's highest and most famous peak, will take your breath away. Climbing it and then watching the sunrise from the summit is one of Japan's superlative experiences. The official climbing season runs from 1 July to 31 August. Outside the climbing season, you can take a bus halfway up the mountain to the Fifth Station or hunt for views from the foothills around the lake, Kawaguchi-ko.

View from Mt Fuji summit at sunrise

Don't Miss

The Fifth Station

The Fifth Station (2305m) on the Kawaguchi-ko trail is where most climbers begin their ascent. Outside the climbing season, from mid-April to early December, you can take a bus (one way/return ¥1540/2100, 50 minutes) from Kawaguchi-ko to the Fifth Station to stand in awesome proximity of the snowcapped cone. There are also impressive views of the surrounding area from here.

The Climb

Most would-be climbers on a short trip opt for an overnight trek, aiming to get to the summit at dawn. Of the four trails, the Kawaguchi-ko trail from Kawaguchi-ko Fifth Station is the most popular route as it's the easiest to reach by public transport from Tokyo. For more details on making the ascent, see www.city.fujiyoshida.yamanashi.jp/div/english/html/climb.html. During the climbing season, buses run directly from Shinjuku to the Fifth Station (¥2700, 2½ hours).

Nearby: Kawaguchi-ko

Nearby Kawaguchi-ko acts as a natural reflecting pool for the mountain's cone. The eponymous lakeside town offers year-round activities including hiking and onsen-soaking. For excellent views, take the **Kachi Kachi Yama Ropeway** (カチカチ山ロープウェイ; www.kachikachiyama-ropeway.com; 1163-1 Azagawa; 1-way/return adult ¥410/720, child ¥210/360; ⊙9am-5pm) to the Fuji Viewing Platform (1104m). If you have time, there is a 3½-hour hike from here to Mitsutōge-yama (三つ峠山; 1785m), which offers more views. Ask at Kawaguchi-ko Tourist Information Center for a map.

☑ Top Tips

▶ The **Kawaguchi-ko Tourist Information Center** (☑0555-72-6700; ⊙8.30am-5.30pm Sun-Fri, to 7pm Sat), next to Kawaguchi-ko Station (where buses also stop), has English-speaking staff, plus maps and brochures.

▶ Weekdays see fewer climbers, except during the week-long O-Bon holiday, in mid-August.

▶ Before deciding to climb, check summit weather at www.snow-forecast.com/resorts/Mount-Fuji.

▶ **Fujisan Hotel** (www.fujisanhotel.com), a mountain hut at the Eighth Station of the Kawaguchi-ko trail, is popular with international climbers.

✕ Take a Break

Hōtō are Kawaguchi-ko's local noodles, hand-cut and served in a thick miso stew. Try them at **Hōtō Fudō** (ほうとう不動; ☑72-8511; www.houtou-fudou.jp; 707 Kawaguchi; hōtō ¥1080; ⊙11am-7pm).

The Best of
Tokyo

Tokyo's Best Walks

Tokyo's Best...

Shinjuku-gyoen (p101)
TOM BONAVENTURE/GETTY IMAGES ©

Best Walks
Contemporary Architecture in Omote-sandō

🏃 The Walk

Omote-sandō is a broad, tree-lined boulevard running between Harajuku and Aoyama. It's known for its parade of upmarket boutiques designed by the who's who of (mostly) Japanese contemporary architects. This stretch of prime real estate functions as a walk-through design showroom and is full of architectural eye candy. All of the buildings on the route are contemporary, though the final stop, Nezu Museum, is a modern take on the traditional Japanese villa.

Start Tokyū Plaza; 🚇 Harajuku

Finish Nezu Museum; 🚇 Omote-sandō

Length 1.5km; one hour

✖ Take a Break

On Omote-sandō, between Harajuku and Aoyama, **Anniversaire Café** (3-5-30 Kita-Aoyama, Minato-ku; 11am-11pm Mon-Fri, 9am-11pm Sat & Sun), has an attractive patio that is perfect for people-watching.

MAEMAGNUM/GETTY IMAGES ©

Omote-sandō, Harajuku (p88)

❶ Tokyū Plaza

Tokyū Plaza (2012) is a castle-like structure by up-and-coming architect Nakamura Hiroshi. The entrance is a dizzying hall of mirrors and there's a spacious roof garden on top.

❷ Omotesandō Hills

Andō Tadao's deceptively deep **Omotesandō Hills** (2003) is a high-end shopping mall spiralling around a sunken central atrium. It replaced an ivy-covered pre-WWII apartment building (to considerable protest); the low horizontal design pays homage to the original structure.

❸ Dior Building

Across the street from Omotesandō Hills, the flagship boutique for **Dior** (2003), designed by Pritzker Prize winner SANAA (composed of Sejima Kazuyo and Nishizawa Ryūe), has a filmy, white exterior that seems to hang like a dress; made entirely of glass and a thin grey sheath, it acts as a semipermeable veil protecting the refined interior from the urban tangle outside.

❹ Louis Vuitton Building

Meant to evoke a stack of clothes trunks, Aoki Jun's design for **Louis Vuitton** (2002) features offset panels of tinted glass behind sheets of metal mesh of varying patterns.

❺ Tod's Building

Climb onto the elevated crosswalk to better admire Itō Toyō's construction for **Tod's** (2004). The criss-crossing strips of concrete take their inspiration from the zelkova trees below; what's more impressive is that they're also structural.

❻ Spiral Building

Maki Fumihiko's postmodernist **Spiral Building** is worth a detour down Aoyama-dōri. Constructed in 1985, it predates everything else on this walk. The patchwork, uncentred design is a nod to Tokyo's own mismatched landscape. Inside, a spiralling passage doubles as an **art gallery**.

❼ Prada Building

The most internationally famous structure on this strip is the convex glass fishbowl that Herzog and de Meuron designed for **Prada** (2003).

❽ Nezu Museum

Finish the walk at the traditional-meets-modern **Nezu Museum** (p88), remodelled in 2009 by Kuma Kengō. The bamboo-lined entrance is likened by the architect to the pathway that leads to a traditional teahouse, which gives the visitor time to adjust their mood.

Best Walks
Asakusa Shitamachi

🏃 The Walk

Shitamachi is the word used to describe parts of Tokyo that come closest to approximating the spirit of old Edo (Tokyo under the shogun). Asakusa is one of those places. Not only does it have important temples and shrines dating to the Edo era (1603–1868) or earlier, but it also has the narrow lanes and wooden shopfronts that characterise Shitamachi today. This walk will take you past the main sights, and also along lanes that ooze old-Tokyo atmosphere.

Start Azuma-bashi; **S** Asakusa

Finish Ef; **S** Asakusa

Length 3km; two hours

✖ Take a Break

Stop for tempura at Daikokuya (p139) – in business since 1887 – on Dembō-in-dōri. You'll also find snack vendors along Nakamise-dōri, such as Chōchin Monaka (p140).

Sensō-ji (p134)

KEREN SU/GETTY IMAGES ©

❶ Azuma-bashi

Originally built in 1774, **Azuma-bashi** was once the departure point for boat trips to the Yoshiwara pleasure district, just north of Asakusa. Today, **tourist boats** go from a nearby pier to Hama-rikyū Onshi-teien and Odaiba (in Tokyo Bay).

❷ Sensō-ji

The grand gate Kaminarimon marks the entrance to the ancient temple **Sensō-ji** (p134), which has been drawing pilgrims to Asakusa for centuries. Also worth a visit is nearby **Asakusa-jinja** (p137), a rare early-Edo Shintō shrine, dating to the early 17th century.

❸ Dembō-in-dōri

Dembō-in-dōri is lined with shops fronted by wooden signboards and sliding doors, providing a historic atmosphere. Stop in **Yonoya Kushiho** (p143), a shop that has been producing boxwood combs since 1717. At the end of the street is **Chingo-dō** (p137), a tiny Buddhist temple dedicated to the *tanuki*, the Japanese raccoon dog.

❹ Hoppy-dōri

Next head up the lane called **Hoppy-dōri**, lined with *yakitori* (chicken, and other meats or vegetables, grilled on skewers) stalls. Go on, have a few skewers and a beer. At the end, you'll pass **Hanayashiki**, Japan's oldest amusement park.

❺ Traditional Crafts Museum

The **Traditional Crafts Museum** (p139) showcases crafts still produced locally in Asakusa, and it's free to enter. It's in one of the neighbourhood's many covered shopping arcades. Keep an eye out for shops selling traditional goods like *geta* (the sandals worn with kimono).

❻ Asakusa Engei Hall

Lantern-lit **Asakusa Engei Hall** (p142) is reminiscent of the vaudeville halls that were once common here. The theatre is part of Asakusa's Rokku district, a famous (and famously bawdy) entertainment district during the century before WWII.

❼ Vintage Shopping

Drop by vintage store **Tokyo Hotarudo** (p142), where the goods pay homage to the early 20th century, when Asakusa was thought of as the Montmartre of Tokyo.

❽ Ef

Finish up at **Ef** (p141), a cafe and gallery in an old wooden building, originally a warehouse dating back to 1868.

Best Walks
Historic Marunouchi & Ginza

🏃 The Walk

Neighbouring Marunouchi and Ginza were the first Tokyo neighbourhoods to modernise (in the Western sense) after Japan opened its doors to foreign influence at the end of the 19th century. Many reminders of this fascinating, turbulent time still exist. This is also where you'll find top sights, such as the Imperial Palace and Kabuki-za, and the city's most expensive real estate.

Start Tokyo Station; 🚉 Tokyo

Finish Kabuki-za; Ⓢ Higashi-Ginza

Length 3km; two hours

✗ Take a Break

Rose Bakery (p29), near the Imperial Palace, does light lunches, coffee and cake. There is also plenty of treats to be sourced from the *depachika* (department store food hall) in Mitsukoshi (p43).

Nijū-bashi and the Imperial Palace (p24)

❶ Tokyo Station

Head out the Marunouchi exit to see the recently restored domes of **Tokyo Station** (p27). Conceived as the city's first rail hub, the European-style brick station opened in 1914.

❷ Marunouchi Building

Walking west from the station, you'll pass the **Marunouchi Building**, first erected in 1923 when Marunouchi was taking shape as the city's first modern business district. The building emerged 30 storeys taller after a renovation in 2001. From the 35th-floor **lounge**, you can see all the way to the Imperial Palace.

❸ Japan Post Tower

The **Japan Post Tower** (2013) is the latest of Marunouchi's early-20th-century buildings to be redone as a skyscraper. The street-level facade evokes the original structure. Inside you'll find the museum, **Intermediateque** (p27).

❹ Imperial Palace

After the Meiji Restoration brought the emperor from Kyoto to Tokyo, the **Imperial Palace** (p24) was built to replace the shogun's castle, Edo-jō. Walk along the moat and look into the distance to see some of the old castle keeps that still remain.

❺ Naka-dōri

From the palace, walk down pretty, tree-lined **Naka-dōri** to Ginza. With boutiques and cafes, this is now one of Tokyo's most fashionable strips.

❻ Ginza

Ginza was the city's first modern retail district, where department stores introduced the latest fashions from the West. At the heart of the neighbourhood is the Yon-chōme intersection, where you'll find the department store **Mitsukoshi** (p154).

❼ Shiseido Gallery

Walk down Ginza's main drag, Chūō-dōri, which is closed to cars on Sunday afternoons, to the lipstick red Shiseido Building. In the basement is **Shiseido Gallery** (p39), one of the city's first contemporary galleries.

❽ Kabuki-za

Tokyo's premier kabuki theatre, **Kabuki-za** (p36), has stood on this spot since 1889 and recently drew headlines for the completion of a lengthy renovation. Stop by to see the contemporary take on the traditional kabuki-theatre facade.

Best
Architecture

FRANK DEMM/GETTY IMAGES ©

Tokyo is forever under construction; there is always something new going up that is taller, sleeker and generally more dazzling than what existed before. It's fertile ground for the country's architects, many of whom are among the most feted in their world. The city's soaring towers, stunning museums and fanciful boutiques will make architecture fans swoon.

Architecture Across the City

During the construction boom in the decades following WWII, Tokyo expanded to the west and this is where you'll see more contemporary structures and the riot of neon that has come to symbolise modern Tokyo. The east side is considered the old city, though few truly old buildings remain. Still, in small pockets, such as around Ueno and Asakusa, you can see some examples of the traditional wooden structures that once defined Tokyo.

Contemporary Design

Tange Kenzō was the most prominent architect of the post-WWII years, creating landmark structures such as the National Gymnasium in Yoyogi-kōen and the Tokyo Metropolitan Government Offices (p101). Among Kenzō's contemporaries were the Metabolists Kurokawa Kishō and Maki Fumihiko, whose design philosophy championed flexible spaces over fixed form.

A second wave of architects arrived in the 1980s and 1990s, who continue to explore both modernism and postmodernism, pushing forward while also drawing on Japan's rich heritage. Names to know include Kuma Kengō and Pritzker Prize winners Andō Tadao, SANAA (Sejima Kazuyo and Nishizawa Ryūe) and Itō Toyō.

☑ **Top Tip**

▶ Omote-sandō is the best place in the city to see contemporary architecture. Here you'll find works from most of the rising stars, all on one strip so that you can easily compare styles. For a walk through the neighbourhood, see p150.

Best Structural Statements

Tokyo Metropolitan Government Offices
Imposing, iconic skyscrapers by Tange Kenzō. (p101)

Nakagin Capsule Tower
Retro vision of the future, by Kurokawa Kishō. (p40)

Tokyo Metropolitan Government Offices

Tokyo International Forum Soaring glass vessel in the heart of downtown. (p27)

Super Dry Hall Phillipe Starck's curious golden plume. (p137)

Roppongi Hills Ambitious, utopian microcity. (p48)

Tokyo Sky Tree Tokyo's newest sky-high landmark. (p137)

Tokyo Station Recently restored 100-year-old station. (p27)

Tokyo Tower Beloved symbol of post-WWII Tokyo. (p52)

Best Museum Architecture

National Art Center Tokyo Sculptural structure of curving glass by Kurokawa Kishō. (p53)

Gallery of Hōryū-ji Treasures Modernist home of ancient Buddhist sculpture, designed by Yoshio Taniguchi. (p122)

21_21 Design Sight Concrete clam shell by Andō Tadao. (p52)

Best East Meets West

Kyū Iwasaki-teien Nineteenth-century estate with both Western- and Japanese-style wings. (p128)

Tokyo Metropolitan Teien Art Museum Art deco former princely residence. (p65)

Takashimaya Opulent 1930s department store filtered through Japanese sensibilities. (p30)

Worth a Trip

On the grounds of a sprawling park, the **Edo-Tokyo Open Air Architecture Museum** (江戸東京たてもの園; www.tate-monoen.jp/english; 3-7-1 Sakura-chō, Koganei-shi; adult/child ¥400/free; ⊙9.30am-5.30pm Tue-Sun Apr-Sep, to 4.30pm Oct-Mar; ℝJR Chūō line to Musashi-Koganei) preserves a number of original structures, from the Edo period (1603–1868) to the early post-WWII years, all rescued from Tokyo's modernising zeal.

Best **Temples & Shrines**

MARE MAGNUM/GETTY IMAGES ©

Tokyo is home to countless Buddhist temples and Shintō shrines, honouring Japan's two entwined religions. The grounds are free to enter and open to all – so long as the gate is open. The grandest ones are simply stunning, but just as enchanting are the tiny temples and shrines tucked among buildings that you're likely to stumble upon as you explore the city.

☑ **Top Tips**

▶ Temples and shrines host festivals throughout the year. For event listings, see Go Tokyo (www. gotokyo.org/en/ index.html).

▶ It is customary to make a small offering at both temples and shrines. Fortunately for budget travellers, a ¥5 coin is considered the luckiest (¥10 coins are unlucky).

Visiting Etiquette

Shrines and temples don't have strict rules (there are no dress codes, for example). However, there are some prescribed manners. Since the *torii* (gates in front of a Shintō shrine) indicate the entrance to sacred space, you'll often see Japanese visitors bowing upon entering and exiting. Before approaching the main shrine, it is customary to wash your hands at the font, since Shintō prizes purity.

Temples often have a slightly raised threshold, which you should step over – not on. Taking pictures on the grounds is fine, but many temples do not want you taking photos – especially flash photos – of the inside.

Best Temples

Sensō-ji Beloved symbol of Tokyo for centuries. (p134)

Zōjō-ji A sprawling temple, home to the tombs of former shoguns. (p53)

Kiyōmizu Kannon-dō Modelled after Kyoto's famous Kiyōmizu-dera. (p127)

Best Shrines

Meiji-jingū Tokyo's grandest shrine, set in a wooded grove. (p84)

Asakusa-jinja Edo-era structure that survived earthquakes, fire and war. (p137)

Yasukuni-jinja Beautiful, controversial shrine

to Japan's war dead. (p113)

Ueno Tōshō-gū Gilded gem in Ueno-kōen. (p127)

Nogi-jinja The scene of General Nogi's famous ritual suicide. (p54)

Best
Parks & Gardens

Apartment-dwellers of Tokyo may not have the luxury of backyards, but they have hectares of open space in the city's many parks – almost all of which are free to enter. Most of the city's sprawling, manicured gardens, which cost just a few hundred yen, once belonged to the imperial family or the former feudal elite.

I AM HAPPY TAKING PHOTOGRAPHS/GETTY IMAGES ©

Cherry Blossoms

Tokyo's parks and gardens come to life during *hanami* (cherry-blossom viewing), which usually happens in late March or early April. Groups of friends and coworkers gather under the *sakura* (cherry blossoms) for sake-drenched picnics. It's a centuries-old tradition, to celebrate the fleeting beauty of life, symbolised by the blossoms which last only a week or two.

Ueno-kōen has long been Tokyo's most famous *hanami* spot. Yoyogi-kōen is where serious party-people come armed with barbecues, karaoke machines and even turntables. Shinjuku-gyoen is a grassy, family-friendly spot for lazing under the blossoms. Naka-Meguro's **Meguro-gawa** (目黒川; [S] Hibiya line to Naka-Meguro), a tree-lined canal, is another local favourite; come in the evening for *yozakura* (night-time cherry blossoms), when the canal is lit with lanterns.

☑ **Top Tip**

▶ Pick up a *bentō* (boxed meal) from a *depachika* (department store food hall) or convenience store for a picnic lunch.

Institute for Nature Study What Tokyo would look like with no people. (p65)

Best Parks

Yoyogi-kōen The city's biggest, liveliest swath of green and a popular gathering spot, especially on weekends. (p88)

Shinjuku-gyoen An imperial garden turned glorious park. (p101)

Ueno-kōen A pond choked with waterlilies, plus temples and shrines. (p127)

Best Gardens

Hama-rikyū Onshi-teien A manicured garden with a centuries-old teahouse. (p39)

Koishikawa Kōrakuen A classic Edo-era landscaped garden. (p113)

Imperial Palace East Garden On the palace grounds, with the ruins of an old stone keep. (p25)

Best
Galleries &
Museums

Tokyo is a city enamoured with museums. Not only does it have many excellent established institutions, it is constantly building new ones. These include both grand repositories of art and antiquities, and tiny centres of devotion to one particular thing. Tokyo is also the centre of Japan's contemporary-art scene and has numerous galleries to show for it.

TRAVEL ASIA/GETTY IMAGES ©

Contemporary-Art Scene

Tokyo's contemporary-art scene is broad, dynamic and scattered – much like the city itself. Ginza is Tokyo's original gallery district. In the last decade, Roppongi, with its three big museums – Mori Art Museum, National Art Center Tokyo and Suntory Museum of Art – has emerged as an arts centre. For public art, look to commercial and office complexes Roppongi Hills and Shinjuku i-Land. Yanaka has long been an artist's neighbourhood and there are galleries and studios there too.

Access & Admission

Many museums close one day a week, often on Mondays (or, if Monday is a national holiday, then the following Tuesday). Museums in Tokyo tend to close early, around 5pm or 6pm, and last admission is 30 minutes before closing. Take advantage of the free lockers (¥100 deposit) to stow your coat and bag. Permanent exhibits at national museums are the most economical; expect to pay more for admission to temporary exhibits or private museums. Concessions are often available for students and seniors; bring ID. Commercial galleries are free to enter.

☑ Top Tip

▶ See p178 for information on museum discounts.

▶ Check out Tokyo Art Beat (www.tokyoartbeat.com) for exhibition listings and reviews. The site also produces a printed guide every other month to the best shows around town; look for it at museums and galleries.

Best Museums

Tokyo National Museum Hands down the best collection of Japanese art and antiquities anywhere. (p122)

Mori Art Museum Blockbuster, large-scale contemporary exhibits. (p49)

Tokyo Metropolitan Museum of Photography The city's best photography museum. (p65)

Ghibli Museum Captures the world of animator Miyazaki Hayao. (p109)

Intermediateque Experimental museum drawing on the holdings of the University of Tokyo. (p27)

Best for Traditional Art

Ukiyo-e Ōta Memorial Art Museum Woodblock prints by masters of the medium. (p88)

Nezu Museum Asian antiquities in a striking contemporary building. (p88)

Best for Contemporary Art

21_21 Design Sight Dedicated to all things design. (p52)

Watari Museum of Contemporary Art Progressive and provocative exhibitions. (p90)

Best for Crafts

Suntory Museum of Art Ceramics, glassware, lacquerware etc from Japan and abroad. (p52)

Crafts Gallery Works from Japan's 'living national treasures'. (p28)

Best History Museums

Shitamachi Museum Re-creation of a wooden, Edo-era tenement neighbourhood. (p128)

National Shōwa Memorial Museum Exhibitions on daily life for the Japanese during WWII. (p113)

Best Galleries

SCAI the Bathhouse Cutting-edge contemporary art in a converted bathhouse. (p125)

Shiseido Gallery One of Ginza's original galleries. (p39)

Best Quirky Museums

Beer Museum Yebisu A concise history of beer in Japan. (p65)

Meguro Parasitological Museum Internal creepy-crawlies on display. (p66)

Worth a Trip

The excellent **Edo-Tokyo Museum** (江戸東京博物館; ☎3626-9974; www.edo-tokyo-museum.or.jp; 1-4-1 Yokoami, Sumida-ku; adult/child ¥600/free; ⏱9.30am-5.30pm Tue-Sun, to 7.30pm Sat; ☒JR Sōbu line to Ryōgoku, west exit) documents Tokyo's epic transition from old Edo (Tokyo under the shogun) to its modern avatar. Highlights include real examples of Edo-era infrastructure and impeccably detailed scale models of markets and shops during the era of the shogun.

Best
Food

When it comes to Tokyo superlatives, the city's eating scene takes the cake. There are more restaurants in this pulsing megalopolis than in any other city in the world. And the quality is unparalleled too – you're rarely more than 500m from a good, if not great, restaurant. Best of all, you can eat well on any budget in pretty much every neighbourhood.

Tokyo Dining Scene

Older neighbourhoods like Ueno and Asakusa are known for their traditional, sometimes century-old, restaurants. Cosmopolitan Roppongi has the most variety in terms of international cuisine. For sushi – a Tokyo speciality – Ginza and Tsukiji are tops; Ginza is also known for its upscale restaurants. Lunch is usually excellent value, with many pricier restaurants offering cheaper courses during the noontime hours. Westside neighbourhoods like Ebisu, Shibuya and Harajuku have more trendy joints. Of course there are a numerous exceptions to all of this too!

The city also has the most cosmopolitan dining scene and is the epicentre of many trends, such as the current fashion for 'standing restaurants' (casual, wallet-friendly joint without seats).

Izakaya

Izakaya (居酒屋) translates as drinking house – the Japanese equivalent of a pub. Here food is ordered for the table a few dishes at a time and washed down with plenty of beer or sake. *Izakaya* come in all stripes, from stripped-down working-class joints to *oshare* (fashionable) date spots. Either way, it's a classic local experience.

PAMELA LAO/GETTY IMAGES ©

☑ Top Tips

▶ Reservations are necessary at high-end restaurants and a good idea at midrange places, especially on weekends or if your party is larger than two.

▶ Traditional or smaller restaurants may not accept credit cards.

▶ Check out Tokyo Food Page (www.bento.com) for dining listings and reviews in English.

Best Japanese

Kikunoi Gorgeous *kaiseki* in the classic Kyoto style. (p54)

Tonki *Tonkatsu* (fried pork cutlets) as art. (p66)

Kado Classic home cooking in a classic old house. (p115)

d47 Shokudō Regional specialities from around the country. (p75)

Best Local Eating

Shirube Wildly popular *izakaya* with inventive dishes. (p81)

Nagi Late-night *rāmen* in Golden Gai. (p99)

Ebisu-yokochō Hip retro dining arcade. (p67)

Best Old-Tokyo Flavour

Hantei Grilled skewers in a 100-year-old heritage house. (p129)

Komagata Dojō One of the few restaurants that still serves stewed eel, an Edo-era dish. (p139)

Omoide-yokochō Atmospheric *yakitori* stalls near the train tracks. (p102)

Best Sushi

Kyūbey Rarefied Ginza sushi at its finest. (p40)

Daiwa Sushi Ultrafresh fish served inside Tsukiji Fish Market. (p40)

Sushi-no-Midori Popular joint selling filling,

reasonably priced sets. (p76)

Best Izakaya

Shinsuke Century-old *izakaya* adored by sake aficionados. (p129)

Jōmon Lively counter joint serving delicious charcoal-grilled skewers. (p55)

Ippo Specialises in fish and sake – what more do you need? (p67)

Best Splurge

Tofuya-Ukai Handmade tofu becomes haute cuisine. (p54)

Matsukiya Melt-in-your-mouth *sukiyaki*. (p76)

Kozue Exquisite Japanese cuisine and stunning views over Shinjuku. (p102)

Best Seafood

Yanmo Extravagant spreads of seafood prepared Japanese-style. (p90)

Trattoria Tsukiji Paradiso! Linguine and clams instead of sushi at Tsukiji Market. (p41)

Best Noodles

Afuri Cult-fave noodle shop with light, citrus broth. (p67)

Tokyo Rāmen Street Mini branches of the country's best *rāmen* shops. (p29)

Best Brunch

Rose Bakery Quiches, tarts and decadent cakes. (p154)

Lauderdale Soufflés, salads and pavement seating. (p55)

Worth a Trip

A 10-minute walk from Naka-Meguro Station and all but hidden in a swanky residential enclave, **Higashi-Yama** (ヒガシヤマ; ☎ 5720-1300; www.higashiyama-tokyo.jp; 1-21-25 Higashiyama, Meguro-ku; lunch/dinner courses from ¥2500/4500; ☻11.30am-2pm Tue-Sat, 6pm-1am Mon-Sat; Ⓢ Hibiya line to Naka-Meguro) serves up gorgeous modern Japanese cuisine in a stark, minimalist setting. Look for the concrete building with the small, illuminated sign.

Best
Sentō & Onsen

Don't be shy! Many Japanese would argue that you couldn't possibly understand their culture without taking a dip, and the blissful relaxation that follows can turn a sceptic into a convert. Onsen (hot springs) are believed to have therapeutic powers. *Sentō* are old-school public bathhouses dating from the era when Tokyo housing didn't have private baths.

DAJ/GETTY IMAGES ©

Bathing Etiquette

Getting naked with strangers is scary enough, so relax. There's really only one hard-and-fast rule you need to remember: wash yourself *before* you get in the bath.

When you enter a bathhouse, put your shoes in a locker at the entrance. Then pay your admission fee and head to the correct – check the characters on the door curtains – changing room. Leave your clothes in a locker or basket and enter the bathing room with just your toiletries and a small hand-towel. Park yourself on a stool in front of one of the taps and give yourself a thorough wash, making sure to rinse off all the suds.

That little towel performs a variety of functions: you can use it to wash (but make sure to give it a good rinse afterwards) or to cover yourself as you walk around. It is not supposed to touch the water though, so leave it on the side of the bath or – as many Japanese do – folded on top of your head. Before heading back to the changing room, use it to wipe yourself down, so as not to drip on the changing-room floor.

Note that many bathhouses refuse entry to persons with tattoos because of their association with the *yakuza* (Japanese mafia).

☑ Top Tips

▶ *Sentō* don't provide soap and towels, so bring your own (or buy some from the counter).

▶ Know your kanji: 女 means women and 男 means men.

Best Baths

Ōedo Onsen Monogatari 'Onsen theme park' with real hot-spring water and a variety of tubs. (p145)

Jakotsu-yu A classic *sentō* with pure hot-spring water and no policy against tattoos. (p137)

Spa LaQua Urban oasis with multiple baths and saunas. (p113)

Best
Traditional
Theatre & Dance

Tokyo, when it was Edo (1603–1868), had a rich theatre culture. Above all, there was kabuki – captivating, occasionally outrageous and beloved by the townspeople. Ribald *rakugo* (comedic monologue) was another favourite diversion in Edo times, and still draws audiences today. Other classic forms include *nō* (stylised dance-drama), *gagaku* (music of the imperial court) and *bunraku* (classic puppet theatre).

WILL ROBB/GETTY IMAGES ©

Kabuki

Though kabuki is centuries old, a day at the theatre is still a popular pastime. In Tokyo, kabuki performances are held at Kabuki-za in Ginza. Shows run for 25 days a month and ticket sales begin on the 12th of the preceding month. A whole performance lasts several hours. If you're on a tight schedule, however, you can opt for a *makumi* ticket (¥800–¥2000) for just one act, lasting about an hour. These tickets are only good for 4th-tier seats.

Rakugo

Rakugo was another popular diversion of the working class in Edo. The performer sits on a square cushion on stage, using only a fan and a hand towel as props. A typical show lasts hours and features many performers. A number of famous comedians, including movie director Kitano Takeshi, have studied *rakugo* as part of their development.

☑ Top Tips

▶ Purchase kabuki tickets from http://www.kabuki-bito.jp/eng/top.html.

▶ Get kabuki *makumi* (single-act) tickets an hour before the show from the counter in front of the theatre.

▶ Rent a headset (¥700, plus ¥1000 deposit) at Kabuki-za for explanations of the plays and dialogue translations. It's impossible to follow without it!

National Nō Theatre
Ancient *nō* on a sparse stage. (p93)

Asakusa Engei Hall An old-fashioned vaudeville stage for *rakugo* comedians, jugglers and more. (p142)

Best Traditional Theatres

Kabuki-za *The* place to go for kabuki. (p36)

National Theatre All forms of traditional theatre. (p58)

Best
Shopping & Markets

Tokyo is the trendsetter for the rest of Japan, and its residents shop – economy be damned – with an infectious enthusiasm. From quirky fashion to cutting-edge electronics, antiques to traditional crafts, Tokyo has many ways to tempt your wallet. Merchandise is generally of excellent quality, and not as wildly expensive as you might think.

FRANK DEIM/GETTY IMAGES ©

Shopping Tokyo

Tokyo is famous for its fashion tribes, each of whom has a preferred stomping ground. Ginza has long been Tokyo's premier shopping district and is home to many high-end department stores and boutiques. Rival Harajuku, on the other side of town, has boutiques that deal in both luxury fashion and street cred. Shibuya is the locus of the teen-fashion trend machine, while nearby Shimo-Kitazawa has the city's highest concentration of vintage-clothing stores. Ebisu and Meguro are known for small one-off shops selling artsy fashions and homewares.

For one-stop shopping, Shinjuku is your best bet: here you'll find department stores, electronics outfitters, book shops, record shops and fashionable boutiques. Akihabara is the place to go to source goods related to anime (Japanese animation) and manga (Japanese comics). Ueno and Asakusa have many stores selling artisan crafts, both traditional and contemporary.

Antiques & Flea Markets

Tokyo's biggest and best antique market is the Ōedo Antique Market (p27), held on the first and third Sunday of the month. Some shrines and temples also host regular flea markets; for listings, see **Metropolis** (http://metropolisjapan.com/events).

☑ **Top Tip**

▶ More and more shops are offering tax-free shopping to foreign tourists who spend more than ¥10,000. Look for the sign in the window and bring your passport. Otherwise tax is 8% (rising to 10% in spring 2017).

Best for Fashion

Sou-Sou Traditional Japanese clothing with contemporary panache. (p94)

Dover Street Market Comme des Garçons and other avant-garde Japanese labels. (p42)

Fake Tokyo Hipster boutique with the latest labels and vintage finds. (p78)

GARY CONNER/GETTY IMAGES ©

Antique dolls for sale

Laforet Harajuku landmark filled with kooky clothes. (p94)

Best Local Shopping

Don Quijote An all-night treasure trove of miscellaneous oddities. (p99)

Meguro Interior Shops Community Tokyo's interior-design district. (p68)

Best for Souvenirs

Tōkyū Hands Cute stationery, lifestyle gadgets and bizarre beauty products. (p78)

Souvenir from Tokyo One-of-a-kinds from local artists and designers. (p59)

RanKing RanQueen All the latest must-haves. (p107)

Best Department Stores

Mitsukoshi Classic department store with an excellent food hall. (p154)

Isetan Tokyo's most fashion-forward department store. (p107)

Best Traditional Shops

Takumi One-stop shop for earthy crafts. (p42)

Musubi Versatile patterned clothes called *furoshiki*. (p94)

Bengara Beautiful linen *noren* (hanging door curtains). (p142)

Best Shopping Streets

Ameya-yokochō Vintage post-WWII market in Ueno. (p127)

Worth a Trip

For proof that Tokyo's centuries-old artisan tradition is still alive and kicking, take a trip to **2K540 Aki-Oka Artisan** (アキオカアルチザン; www.jrtk.jp/2k540; 5-9-23 Ueno, Taitō-ku; ⏰11am-7pm Thu-Tue; 🚇Ginza line to Suehirochō, exit 2). In this minimalist bazaar, set up under the JR Yamanote-line tracks between Akihabara and Okachimachi Stations, you'll find young creators peddling all kinds of handmade wares.

Best
Nightlife & Live Music

Tokyo's nightlife is one of the city's highlights. Whatever stereotypes you may have held about Japanese people being quiet and reserved will fall to pieces after dark. Tokyo is a work-hard, play-hard kind of place and you'll find people out any night of the week. There is truly something for everyone here, from sky-high lounges to grungy hole-in-the-walls.

CHRIS MELLOR/GETTY IMAGES ©

What's Hot Now

In the last few years, the craft-beer scene has exploded in and around Tokyo, producing a number of respected breweries and beer bars, such as Good Beer Faucets (p77) and Harajuku Taproom (p92). Another recent trend is the rise of the *tachinomi-ya* (literally 'standing bar'), small, lively joints where patrons crowd around the bar. Karaoke remains ever popular in the land of its birth; to learn more about this very Japanese pastime, see p106.

It's not all about the booze: Tokyo has an ever-growing number of fantastic coffee houses too.

Clubbing & Live Music

Tokyo has a healthy club scene, centred mostly around Shibuya and Roppongi. Friday and Saturday are the big nights out, though most clubs have something going on nearly every night. Discount flyers can be downloaded from most club websites. While bars don't ask for ID, clubs do: you must be 20 to enter and you *must* have a picture ID – even if you are decades beyond 20.

Tokyo's home-grown live-music scene has turned out some good acts, often found playing around Shibuya, Ebisu and Shimo-Kitazawa. See **Tokyo Dross** (http://tokyodross.blogspot.jp/) for a list of the month's best gigs.

☑ **Top Tip**

▶ Get tickets for concerts at **Ticket Pia** (チケットぴあ; ☎ 0570-02-9111; http://t.pia.jp; ⏰ 10am-8pm), on the 4th floor of Shibuya Hikarie (p75) and inside the Asakusa Culture Tourist Information Center (p181).

Best Bars

Buri The *tachinomi-ya* that started the trend. (p68)

Zoetrope The best selection of Japanese whisky in the world. (p104)

Pink Cow Funky wine bar with regular art events. (p56)

Nakame Takkyū Lounge Hip hang-out with a table-tennis table. (p68)

Kagaya Fun and games in an *izakaya* with the incomparable Mark-san. (p41)

Best Local Drinking

Golden Gai A cluster of tiny bars housed in a former black market. (p99)

Never Never Land Groovy Shimo-Kitazawa hideaway. (p81)

These Cocktails and books in posh enclave Nishi-Azabu. (p58)

Nonbei-yokochō Atmospheric alley near the train tracks in Shibuya. (p77)

Best Drinks with a View

New York Bar Sophisticated perch atop the Park Hyatt Hotel. (p106)

Two Rooms Comfy sofas on a terrace overlooking Harajuku. (p92)

Asahi Sky Room Views of Tokyo Sky Tree and the Sumida-gawa. (p142)

Best Clubs

Womb It's all about the music – house and techno – at Tokyo's most famous club. (p77)

SuperDeluxe Artsy lounge with live music and DJ'd events. (p56)

Air House and techno rule at this local fave. (p68)

Best for Live Rock & Pop

WWW Tokyo's hottest, multigenre music space, in a former art-house cinema. (p78)

Unit Basement venue with a consistently great line-up of indie bands, local and international. (p69)

Best for Live Jazz

Shinjuku Pit Inn Straight up, Tokyo's best jazz club. (p107)

STB 139 Classy venue for local and international acts. (p58)

Best for Karaoke

Festa Iikura Fancy dress + karaoke = fab night out. (p56)

'Cuzn Homeground Offering a wild night of warbling in Asakusa. (p141)

Best Cafes

Bear Pond Espresso Syrupy espresso with a devout following. (p81)

Cafe de l'Ambre Classic old coffee shop with hand-roasted beans. (p42)

Worth a Trip

Jicoo The Floating Bar (ジークザフローティングバー; ☎0120-049-490; www.jicoofloatingbar.com; admission ¥2600; ⏰8-10.30pm Thu-Sat; 🚇Yurikamome line to Hinode or Odaiba Kaihin-kōen) cruises around Tokyo Bay after dark in a boat straight out of a sci-fi flick – it's designed by manga (Japanese comics) artist Leiji Matsumoto. DJs and the occasional live act lend a clubby vibe. Naturally, space is limited; reservations recommended.

Best
Pop Culture

ED NORTON/GETTY IMAGES ©

From giant robots to saucer-eyed schoolgirls to a certain ubiquitous kitty, Japanese pop culture is a massive phenomenon that has reached far around the world. At the centre of the manga (Japanese comics) and anime (Japanese animation) vortex is the neighbourhood of Akihabara. For eye-popping street fashion, look to Shibuya and Harajuku.

Akihabara Otaku

Otaku gets translated as 'geek' but it is often used to describe someone who is passionately obsessed with something. More often than not that passion is anime or manga, but it can also mean a devoted fan of a pop idol or a meticulous collector of model trains. The *otaku's* natural habitat is Akihabara, where comic bookshops, cosplay (costume play) cafes and electronics outfitters come together in a blaze of neon.

Shibuya Pop

Shibuya is the centre of Tokyo's teen culture. Here, the latest fashion trends grow legs, pop stars perform on giant TV screens, and nightclubs and karaoke parlours glow all night long.

Harajuku Fashion

Harajuku continues to turn out fascinating fashion tribes, from the *goth-loli* (think zombie Little Bo Peep) of the last decade to today's *doli-kei* (doll-style) girls, who model their look after cherub-cheeked dolls.

Best Pop-Culture Experiences

Shibuya Crossing
Intersection at the heart of Shibuya lit by giant TV screens. (p74)

@Home Cafe Akihabara's most famous maid cafe, where the waitresses dress like French maids. (p119)

Super Potato Retro-kan Old-school video arcade in Akihabara. (p119)

Robot Restaurant Shinjuku cabaret costarring giant robots. (p106)

Purikura no Mecca Arcade with lots of *purikura* (print club) photo booths. (p74)

Takeshita-dōri Harajuku's famous teenage subculture bazaar. (p88)

Best Pop-Culture Shopping

Mandarake Complex Mammoth anime and manga shop. (p119)

Shibuya 109 Teen-fashion trend factory. (p78)

KiddyLand Four-storey emporium of cute character goods. (p94)

Best
Gay & Lesbian

AFP/STRINGER/GETTY IMAGES ©

Tokyo is more tolerant of homosexuality and alternative lifestyles than most of its Asian counterparts, though you won't see public displays of affection, or even hand-holding. Shinjuku-nichōme (nicknamed 'Ni-chōme') is the city's gay and lesbian enclave, where hundreds of establishments are crammed into a space of a few blocks, including bars, dance clubs, saunas and love hotels.

Events & Parties

Tokyo Rainbow Pride (http://tokyorainbowpride.com/), Japan's largest GLBT festival, takes place in April and includes a colourful parade through the streets of Harajuku and Shibuya. The **Tokyo International Lesbian & Gay Film Festival** (www.tokyo-lgff.org), which has been going strong for more than two decades, usually hits the screen in July.

Since most Ni-chōme bars are teeny-tiny, larger events are held at venues around town (you'll spot plenty of flyers in bars around Ni-chōme). **Shangri-La** (www.ageha.com/gn/ja/events/index.html) is arguably the city's best gay party, held roughly every other month at bayside super club Ageha. Another long-running fete is **Fancy Him** (www.fancyhim.com), which draws a mixed straight and gay crowd, often dressed in wild handmade costumes. **Goldfinger** (www.goldfingerparty.com) is Tokyo's sexiest women-only party.

☑ Top Tips

▶ Not all Ni-chōme bars welcome foreigners, ask around or check out Utopia Asia (www.utopia-asia.com) for a list of friendly places (and a handy map).

▶ Love hotels outside Ni-chōme have been known, on occasion, to turn away (or grossly overcharge) same-sex couples; ordinary hotels won't bat an eye.

Best Bars & Clubs

Advocates Cafe A Ni-chōme landmark and the best place to start the night. (p105)

Arty Farty Popular, foreigner-friendly dance club for guys and gals alike. (p106)

Kingyo Irreverent drag revue in Roppongi. (p58)

Best
For Kids

In many ways, Tokyo is a parent's dream: hyperclean, safe and with every mod con. The downside is that most of the top attractions aren't that appealing to little ones. Older kids and teens, however, should get a kick out of Tokyo's pop culture and neon streetscapes. Shibuya and Harajuku in particular are packed with the shops, restaurants and arcades that local teens love.

TRAVEL LINK/GETTY IMAGES ©

Travelling with Children

In central Tokyo (where few families live) large chains (such as Jonathan's, Royal Host and Gusto) are the most family-friendly eating options: they have large booths, high chairs, non-smoking sections and children's menus (usually with Western food). Most hotels have cots for a small fee, but it's near impossible to find a room with two double beds (that isn't an expensive suite). Ryokan (traditional inns) usually have rooms that can accommodate four or five people on futons.

Family Fun

Onsen theme park Ōedo Onsen Monogatari (p144) has a festival atmosphere with old-fashioned games – plus the chance to dress up in *yukata* (light, cotton kimono). Make the most of a rainy afternoon with a trip to a karaoke parlour. Take your little train fans to the southern terrace at Shinjuku Station to watch the world's busiest train station in action.

Best Kid-Friendly Museums

Ghibli Museum Peek inside the world of animator Miyazaki Hayao (*Ponyo*, *Spirited Away*). (p109)

National Science Museum Filled with natural wonders and hands-on activities. (p129)

Tokyo National Museum Samurai armour and swords. (p122)

☑ Top Tips

▶ Children under 12 get in for free at most city museums and gardens.

▶ Kids under six ride for free on public transport; under-12s are charged half the adult fare.

▶ Try to limit your subway time to the hours between 10am and 5pm, when they're free of pushing crowds.

▶ For nursing and nappy-changing stations, department stores are your best bet.

Shitamachi Museum Edo-era games and buildings to explore. (p128)

Survival Guide

Survival Guide

Before You Go

When to Go

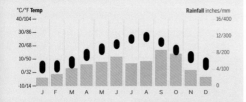

°C/°F Temp
40/104 —
30/86 —
20/68 —
10/50 —
0/32 —
-10/14 —

Rainfall inches/mm
16/400
12/300
8/200
4/100
0

J F M A M J J A S O N D

➡ **Winter (Dec–Feb)**
Cold but clear. December is lively with end-of-year celebrations; the city shuts down for the New Year holiday (1–3 January).

➡ **Spring (Mar–May)**
Gradually warmer days; glorious cherry blossoms from late March to early April.

➡ **Summer (Jun–Aug)**
Rainy season from June to mid-July, then hot and humid. City gets sleepy during the week-long O-Bon holiday in mid-August.

➡ **Autumn (Sep–Nov)**
Warm days turn crisp and cool, with the odd typhoon in September and gorgeous autumn leaves in late November.

Book Your Stay

➡ Tokyo accommodation runs the gamut from sumptuous luxury hotels to cheap dorm rooms in converted warehouses.

➡ Boutique hotels haven't really taken off in Tokyo; instead, ryokan (traditional inns) fill the need for small-scale lodgings with heaps of character. Ueno is the best neighbourhood for ryokan.

➡ Asakusa is Tokyo's backpacker neighbourhood with the highest concentration of hostels.

➡ 'Business hotels' are functional midrange options that exist in every major hub, including Shinjuku and Shibuya – two neighbourhoods that make convenient bases.

➡ Advance booking is highly recommended. You'll get a better price at most hotels, and even at hostels walk-ins can fluster staff.

➡ Note that some mid-range and budget options do not accept credit cards.

Useful Websites

Jalan (www.jalan.net) Popular Japanese discount online booking site.

Japanese Inn Group (www.japaneseinngroup.com) Bookings for ryokan and other family-run inns.

JAPANiCAN (www.japanican.com) Online booking site for foreign travellers run by JTB, Japan's largest travel agency.

Lonely Planet (www.lonelyplanet.com/japan/tokyo/hotels) Author-recommended reviews and online booking.

Best Budget

Nui (http://backpackersjapan.co.jp/nui_en) Hipster hostel in a former warehouse near Asakusa.

Khaosan World (www.khaosan-tokyo.com/en/world/) Trippy hostel in a former love hotel in Asakusa.

Toco (http://backpackersjapan.co.jp) Hostel in a charming old wooden house near Ueno.

Kimi Ryokan (www.kimi-ryokan.jp) Welcoming budget ryokan in northwest Tokyo.

Best Midrange

Claska (www.claska.com/en/hotel) Designer digs in a quiet residential neighbourhood south of Meguro.

Hotel S (http://hr-roppongi.jp) Stylish boutique hotel down the road from Roppongi's nightlife.

Shibuya Granbell (www.granbellhotel.jp) Funky boutique hotel in the thick of Shibuya.

Mitsui Garden Hotel Ginza Premier (www.gardenhotels.co.jp) A great deal in upmarket, centrally located Ginza.

Best Top End

Park Hyatt (http://tokyo.park.hyatt.com) Palatial high-rise with otherworldly views in Shinjuku.

Ritz-Carlton Tokyo (www.ritzcarlton.com) Ultraluxe perch in Roppongi.

Palace Hotel Tokyo (www.palacehoteltokyo.com) Elegant rooms alongside the Imperial Palace in Marunouchi.

Tokyo Station Hotel (www.tokyostationhotel.jp) Classic luxury inside Tokyo Station.

Best Ryokan

Sawanoya Ryokan (www.sawanoya.com) A gem in quiet Yanaka with wonderful hospitality and traditional baths.

Hōmeikan (www.homeikan.com) Beautifully crafted, 100-year-old wooden ryokan, near Ueno.

Sukeroku no Yado Sadachiyo (www.sadachiyo.co.jp) Gorgeous old-world oasis in Asakusa.

Annex Katsutarō Ryokan (www.katsutaro.com) Modern ryokan with friendly managers in Yanaka.

Arriving in Tokyo

☑ **Top Tip** For the best way to get to your accommodation, see p17.

Narita Airport

Narita Airport (成田空港, NRT; ☎0476-34-8000; www.narita-airport.jp) is 66km east of Tokyo.

➔ **Narita Express** (成田 エクスプレス, N'EX; www. jreast.co.jp/e/nex) trains run approximately every half-hour, 7.30am to 9.45pm, to Tokyo Station (¥3020, 53 minutes), with branches heading to Shinjuku, Shibuya or Shinagawa stations (all ¥3110, 1½ hours). Seats are reserved, but tickets can be purchased immediately before departure, if available, from ticket counters near the arrival gate in either terminal. At the time of writing, Japan Rail was offering discount return N'EX tickets for foreign tourists (¥4000, valid for 14 days); inquire at the JR East Travel Service centres at Narita Airport.

➔ **Keisei Skyliner** (京成 スカイライナー; www. keisei.co.jp/keisei/tetudou/ skyliner/us) trains zip twice an hour, 8am to 10.15pm, to Ueno Station (¥2400, 45 minutes), where you can pick up the subway. Trains also stop at Nippori Station for transfers to the JR Yamanote line. Get tickets from the counter at Narita Keisei Station in either terminal. The Skyliner & Tokyo Subway Ticket (¥2800 to ¥3500), which combines a one-way ticket on the

Skyliner and a one-, two- or three-day subway pass, is a good deal.

➔ **Limousine Bus** (リムジンバス; www.limousinebus. co.jp/en) coaches depart regularly from Narita, 7am to 10.30pm, for major hotels and train stations such as Shinjuku (¥3150, 1½ hours). There are ticket counters near the arrival gates at both terminals.

➔ **Taxis** run about ¥30,000 from Narita to the city centre – naturally we don't recommend this.

Haneda Airport

On the southern edge of Tokyo, **Haneda Airport** (羽田空港, HND; 📞 international terminal 6428-0888; www.tokyo-airport-bldg.co.jp/en) is much more convenient than Narita.

➔ **Tokyo Monorail** (東京モノレール; www. tokyo-monorail.co.jp/ english) runs frequently, 5.15am to midnight, to Hamamatsuchō Station (¥490, 15 minutes), where you can transfer to the JR Yamanote line.

➔ **Keikyū Line** (📞5789-8686; www. haneda-tokyo-access.com/ en) airport express trains

run frequently, 5.20am to midnight, from Keikyū Haneda Station to Shinagawa Station (¥410, 12 minutes), where you can transfer to the JR Yamanote line.

➔ A taxi to the city centre – your only option if you opt for a flight that gets in before dawn – averages about ¥6000.

Tokyo Station

Tokyo Station is the terminus for the *shinkansen* (bullet train).

Connect here to the JR Yamanote line or the Marunouchi subway line for points around the city centre, from 5am to midnight.

Getting Around

Bicycle

☑ **Best for...** exploring local neighbourhoods.

➔ Cycling is an excellent way to get around fringe neighbourhoods, though the traffic is not for the faint of heart.

➔ Some budget accommodation (especially around Ueno and

Train Passes

Getting a prepaid train pass – the interchangeable Suica and Pasmo – is highly recommended, even for a short trip. With this card, fitted with an electromagnetic chip, you'll be able to breeze through the ticket gates of any train or subway station in the city without having to work out fares or transfer tickets. Get one from any ticket vending machine (Suica from JR line machines and Pasmo from subway and commuter-line machines); note that the cards require a ¥500 deposit, refundable when you return it to a station window. To use the card, simply wave it over the card reader; you will need to do this to exit the station too.

One-day train and subway passes are available too (¥710 to ¥1590, depending if you ride only Tokyo Metro or also Toei subway lines and JR lines). These only make sense if you plan to cover a lot of ground in one day. For details, see: www.tokyometro.jp/en/ticket/value/1day/.

Asakusa) have bicycles to lend or know where you can rent one.

➡ See **Rentabike** (http://rentabike.jp) for a list of places around town that rent bikes.

Boat

☑ **Best for...** combining sightseeing with transport.

Tokyo Cruise (水上バス, Suijō Bus; ☏ 0120-977-311; http://suijobus.co.jp) water buses run up and down the Sumida-gawa (Sumida River), roughly twice an hour between 10am and 6pm, connecting Asakusa with Hama-rikyū Onshi-teien (¥740, 35 minutes) and Odaiba (¥1560, 50 minutes). Tickets can be purchased immediately before departure, if available, at any pier.

Taxi

☑ **Best for...** late nights and groups sharing the cost.

➡ Flagfall is ¥730. After 2km the meter starts to clock an additional ¥90 for every 280m (and up to ¥90 for every two minutes you sit idly in traffic). It adds up quickly.

➡ Most, but not all, taxis take credit cards.

➡ Look for taxi ranks in front of major train stations and hotels.

➡ You can hail a cab from the street. Taxis with their indicator in red are free; green means taken.

➡ Cabbies usually don't speak English and have trouble finding all but the most well-known spots. Fortunately many have GPS systems, so have an address or a business card for your destination handy.

Train & Subway

☑ **Best for...** getting around the city efficiently.

➡ Tokyo's train network runs approximately 5am to midnight and includes Japan Rail (JR) lines, 13 subway lines – four operated by Toei and nine by Tokyo Metro – and numerous private commuter lines.

➡ Try to avoid rush hour (around 8am to 9.30am and 5pm to 8pm), when 'packed in like sardines' is an understatement.

➡ Tickets are sold from vending machines near the automated ticket gates. Newer touch-screen machines have an English option.

➡ Fares are determined by how far you ride; there should be a fare chart above the ticket machines. If your journey involves lines run by different operators, you'll need to purchase a transfer ticket.

➡ If you can't work out how much to pay, one easy trick is to buy a ticket at the cheapest fare and use one of the 'fare adjustment' machines, near the exit gates, to settle the difference at the end of your journey.

➡ You'll need a valid train ticket to exit the station, so make sure to pick it up when it pops out of the entry gates.

➡ Figure out the best route to your destination with the app **Navitime for Japan Travel** (www.navitime.co.jp/pcstorage/html/japan_travel/english); you can download routes to be used offline too.

➡ Most train stations have multiple exits. Look for maps in the station that show which exits are closest to major area landmarks.

Essential Information

Business Hours

Banks 9am to 3pm Monday to Friday

Bars 5pm to late Monday to Saturday

Boutiques noon to 8pm

Clubs 10pm to 5am Thursday to Saturday

Department stores 10am to 8pm

Museums 9am to 5pm Tuesday to Sunday

Post offices 9am to 5pm Monday to Friday

Restaurants lunch 11.30am to 2.30pm, dinner 6pm to 10pm; larger restaurants stay open throughout the afternoon

Discount Cards

Grutt Pass (www.rekibun.or.jp/grutto; pass ¥2000) A good deal if you plan to hit a lot of museums. Valid for two months, it offers discounted – and sometimes free – admission to more than 70 museums in greater Tokyo; purchase at any affiliated museum.

Electricity

100V/50Hz

Emergency

☑ **Top Tip** Most emergency operators don't speak English, but they will immediately refer you to someone who does.

Ambulance (救急車, Kyūkyūsha; ☎119)

Fire (消防署, Shōbōsho; 📞119)

Police (警視庁, Keishichō; 📞emergency 110, general 3501-0111; www.keishicho. metro.tokyo.jp) Twenty-four-hour staffed *kōban* (police boxes) are located near most major train stations.

Japan Helpline (📞0570-000-911; www.jhelp.com/en/ jhlp.html; ⏱24hr) English-speaking operators can help you negotiate tricky situations, like dealing with the police or hospitals.

Medical Information & Emergency Interpretation (📞emergency translation 5285-8185, medical info 5285-8181; www. himawari.metro.tokyo.jp/qq/ qq13enmnlt.asp; ⏱medical info 9am-8pm, emergency translation 5-8pm Mon-Fri, 9am-8pm Sat & Sun) In English, Chinese, Korean, Thai and Spanish.

Money

☑ **Top Tip** Major hotels, restaurants and shops usually take credit cards. Still, it's a good idea to have cash as backup.

The unit of currency is the Japanese yen (¥).

ATMs

➡ Post offices and 7-Eleven convenience stores have ATMs with English instructions that work with overseas cards; 7-Elevens are open 24 hours.

➡ Most Japanese bank ATMs don't accept foreign-issued cards. The exceptions are **Citibank** (シティバンク; www. citibank.co.jp/en), which has 24-hour ATMs (in English) in Shinjuku, Shibuya, Ginza and Roppongi, and select branches of **Mizuho** (www. mizuhobank.co.jp).

Changing Money

➡ Most banks and some major hotels and department stores can change cash or travellers cheques.

➡ US dollars and euros are the easiest to change and fetch the best rates.

Tipping

➡ Tipping is not standard practice in Japan; however, a service charge (10%) will be added to the bill at upper-end restaurants.

Public Holidays

☑ **Top Tip** When a public holiday falls on a Sunday, the following Monday is taken as a holiday. If a business remains open on a holiday – often the case with museums – then it will usually close the next day.

New Year's Day 1 January

Coming-of-Age Day Second Monday in January

National Foundation Day 11 February

Money-Saving Tips

➡ Many of Tokyo's more expensive restaurants are comparatively reasonable at lunch; you'll get better value if you splurge at midday.

➡ After 5pm, grocery stores, bakeries and even department store food halls slash prices on *bentō* (boxed meals), baked goods and sushi.

➡ Check out **Tokyo Cheapo** (http://tokyocheapo. com) for other suggestions on saving money in Tokyo.

Spring Equinox 21 March

Shōwa Emperor's Day
29 April

Constitution Day 3 May

Green Day 4 May

Children's Day 5 May

Marine Day Third Monday
in July

Mountain Day 11 August,
starting in 2016

**Respect-for-the-Aged
Day** Third Monday in
September

Autumn Equinox Day
22 or 23 September

Sports Day Second
Monday in October

Culture Day 3 November

**Labour Thanksgiving
Day** 23 November

Emperor's Birthday
23 December

Safe Travel

☑ **Top Tip** Crimes against
foreign tourists are ex-
ceedingly rare. That said,
you should exercise the
same caution you would
in your home country.

➡ In the summer of 2014,
Tokyo experienced a rare
outbreak of dengue fever.
It's unclear whether den-
gue will become a regular
presence; however, if you
see barriers blocking
the entrance to a park or

signs with a picture of a
mosquito, stay away.

➡ Touts for bars and
clubs in Roppongi and
Shinjuku's Kabukichō can
be aggressive. Be wary
of following them; while
not common, spiked
drinks followed by theft,
or worse, assault, have
occurred. Overcharging is
the more likely outcome.

➡ Women should note
that *chikan* (gropers) do
haunt crowded trains.
During rush hour, many
trains have women-only
cars (marked in pink).

Telephone

Country code 81

**International access
code** 001

Calling Tokyo

➡ Tokyo's area code is 03,
followed by an eight-digit
number.

➡ Drop the zero from the
area code when calling
Tokyo from abroad.

International Calls

➡ Phonecards with
English instructions are
available from many
convenience stores and
are the most convenient
way to call either locally
or internationally.

Mobile Phones

➡ Overseas mobile
phones are not compat-
ible with local SIM cards.

➡ **B-Mobile** (www.
bmobile.ne.jp/english) rents
data-only SIM cards for
unlocked smart phones
or other internet devices.

➡ **Rentafone Japan**
(📞 from overseas 81-75-212-
0842, toll free within Japan
0120-746-487; www.renta-
fonejapan.com) rents basic
mobiles for ¥3900 a
week (plus ¥300 for each
additional day); domestic
calls cost a reasonable
¥35 per minute.

Payphones

➡ Payphones (usu-
ally bright green) are still
fairly common around
train stations; domestic
calls cost ¥10 per minute.

Toilets

☑ **Top Tip** Public toilets
stocked with toilet paper
are easy to come by and
are almost always clean.
All train stations have
them.

➡ Traditional squat toilets
still exist in Tokyo, but
most places have at least
one Western-style toilet.

➡ You'll see people drying
their hands on handker-
chiefs or small wash-

cloths as most public toilets lack paper towels or hand-dryers; pick one up at a ¥100 shop.

➡ If you encounter one of Japan's state-of-the-art 'washlets' (toilets with bidets), check the control panel for your flush options – 大 means 'big' and 小 means 'small'.

Tourist Information

☑ **Top Tip** Tourist-information centres (TICs) at both terminals at Narita Airport and at the international terminal at Haneda Airport have English-speaking staff who can help you get oriented.

Asakusa Culture Tourist Information Center (浅草文化観光センター; Map p136; ☑ 3842-5566; http://taitonavi.jp; 2-18-9 Kaminarimon, Taitō-ku; ⏰ 9am-8pm; 📶; **S** Ginza line to Asakusa, exit 2) Run by Taitō-ku, this TIC has lots of info on Asakusa and Ueno and a Pia ticket counter, near the entrance to Sensō-ji.

JNTO Tourist Information Center (Map p26; ☑ 3201-3331; www.jnto.go.jp; 1st fl, Shin-Tokyo Bldg, 3-3-1 Marunouchi, Chiyoda-ku; ⏰ 9am-5pm; 📶; 🚃 JR Yamanote line to Yūrakuchō, Tokyo International Forum exit) Run by the Japan National Tourism Organisation (JNTO), this TIC has information on Tokyo and beyond.

JR East Travel Service Center (JR東日本訪日旅行センター; Map p26; www.jreast.co.jp/e/customer_support/service_center_tokyo.html; Tokyo Station, 1-9-1 Marunouchi, Chiyoda-ku; ⏰ 7.30am-8.30pm; 📶; 🚃 JR Yamanote line to Tokyo, Marunouchi north exit) Tourist information, luggage storage, money exchange and bookings for ski and onsen (hot springs) getaways. There are branches in the two airports too.

Tokyo Tourist Information Center (東京観光情報センター; Map p100; ☑ 5321-3077; www.gotokyo.org; 1st fl, Tokyo Metropolitan Government Bldg 1, 2-8-1 Nishi-Shinjuku, Shinjuku-ku;

Dos & Don'ts

➡ Relax. Japan is famous for its hair-splitting etiquette rules, but foreign tourists are given a pass for just about everything.

➡ Pack light. Tokyo hotel rooms tend to be tiny, leaving little room for a big suitcase.

➡ Dress smart if you want to blend in, although for all but the fanciest restaurants, casual clothes are fine.

➡ Wear shoes you can slip on and off easily, as many ryokan and restaurants still ask you to leave your shoes at the door.

➡ Refrain from eating on the subway or while walking down the street – it's considered impolite.

➡ Get in line. The Japanese are famous for forming neat, orderly lines for everything.

🕙9.30am-6.30pm; ⓢ Ōedo line to Tochōmae, exit A4) Combine a trip to the observatories at the Tokyo Metropolitan Government Offices with a stop at the city's official TIC.

Travellers with Disabilities

➡ Newer or recently renovated buildings have ramps, elevators and barrier-free facilities. Still, visitors in wheelchairs will find navigating train stations and crowded city streets a challenge.

➡ **Accessible Japan** (www.tesco-premium.co.jp/aj), though not updated regularly, details the accessibility of hundreds of sites in Tokyo, including hotels, sights and department stores.

➡ For a list of barrier-free hotels, see www.gotokyo.org/en/administration/barrier_free.

Visas

Citizens of 61 countries, including Australia, Canada, Hong Kong, Korea, New Zealand, Singapore, USA, UK and almost all European nations do not require visas to enter Japan for stays of 90 days or less. Consult www.mofa.go.jp/j_info/visit/visa/short/novisa.html for a complete list of visa-exempt countries.

Language

Japanese pronunciation is easy for English speakers, as most of its sounds are also found in English. Note though that it's important to make the distinction between short and long vowels, as vowel length can change the meaning of a word. The long vowels (**ā, ē, ī, ō, ū**) should be held twice as long as the short ones. All syllables in a word are pronounced fairly evenly in Japanese. If you read our pronunciation guides as if they were English, you'll be understood.

To enhance your trip with a phrasebook, visit **lonelyplanet.com**.

Basics

Hello.
こんにちは。 kon·ni·chi·wa

Goodbye.
さようなら。 sa·yō·na·ra

Yes.
はい。 hai

No.
いいえ。 ī·e

Please.
ください。 ku·da·sai

Thank you.
ありがとう。 a·ri·ga·tō

Excuse me.
すみません。 su·mi·ma·sen

Sorry.
ごめんなさい。 go·men·na·sai

How are you?
お元気ですか? o·gen·ki des ka

Fine. And you?
はい、元気です。 hai, gen·ki des
あなたは? a·na·ta wa

Do you speak English?
英語が ē·go ga
話せますか? ha·na·se·mas ka

I don't understand.
わかりません。 wa·ka·ri·ma·sen

Eating & Drinking

I'd like to reserve a table for (two).
(2人)の (fu·ta·ri) no
予約をお yo·ya·ku o
願いします。 o·ne·gai shi·mas

I'd like (the menu).
(メニュー) (me·nyū)
をお願いします。 o o·ne·gai shi·mas

I don't eat (red meat).
(赤身の肉) (a·ka·mi no ni·ku)
は食べません。 wa ta·be·ma·sen

That was delicious!
おいしかった。 oy·shi·kat·ta

Please bring the bill.
お勘定 o·kan·jō
をください。 o ku·da·sai

Cheers!	乾杯!	kam·pai
beer	ビール	bī·ru
coffee	コーヒー	kō·hī

Shopping

I'd like ...
…をください。 ... o ku·da·sai

I'm just looking.
見ているだけです。 mi·te i·ru da·ke des

How much is it?
いくらですか？　　i·ku·ra des ka

That's too expensive.
高すぎます。　　ta·ka·su·gi·mas

Can you give me a discount?
ディスカウント　　dis·kown·to
できますか？　　de·ki·mas ka

Emergencies

Help!
たすけて！　　tas·ke·te

Go away!
離れろ！　　ha·na·re·ro

Call the police!
警察を呼んで！　　kē·sa·tsu o yon·de

Call a doctor!
医者を呼んで！　　i·sha o yon·de

I'm lost.
迷いました。　　ma·yoy·mash·ta

I'm ill.
私は病　　wa·ta·shi wa
気です。　　byō·ki des

Where are the toilets?
トイレは　　toy·re wa
どこですか？　　do·ko des ka

Time & Numbers

What time is it?
何時ですか？　　nan·ji des ka

It's (10) o'clock.
(10)時です。　　(jū)·ji des

Half past (10).
(10)時半です。　　(jū)·ji han des

morning	朝	a·sa
afternoon	午後	go·go
evening	夕方	yū·ga·ta

yesterday	きのう	ki·nō
today	今日	kyō
tomorrow	明日	a·shi·ta

1	一	i·chi
2	二	ni
3	三	san
4	四	shi/yon
5	五	go
6	六	ro·ku
7	七	shi·chi/na·na
8	八	ha·chi
9	九	ku/kyū
10	十	jū

Transport & Directions

Where's the ...?
…はどこ　　... wa do·ko
ですか？　　des ka

What's the address?
住所は何　　jū·sho wa nan
ですか？　　des ka

Can you show me (on the map)?
(地図で)教えて　　(chi·zu de) o·shi·e·te
くれませんか？　　ku·re·ma·sen ka

When's the next (bus)?
次の(バス)は　　tsu·gi no (bas) wa
何時ですか？　　nan·ji des ka

Does it stop at ...?
…に　　... ni
停まりますか？　　to·ma·ri·mas ka

Please tell me when we get to ...
… に着いたら　　...ni tsu·i·ta·ra
教えてください。　　o·shi·e·te ku·da·sai

Behind the Scenes

Send Us Your Feedback

We love to hear from travellers – your comments help make our books better. We read every word, and we guarantee that your feedback goes straight to the authors. Visit **lonelyplanet.com/contact** to submit your updates and suggestions.

Note: We may edit, reproduce and incorporate your comments in Lonely Planet products such as guidebooks, websites and digital products, so let us know if you don't want your comments reproduced or your name acknowledged. For a copy of our privacy policy visit lonelyplanet.com/privacy.

Rebecca's Thanks

A big thanks to my mom for her company and to my husband for his tireless support. To my wonderful friends Emi, Steph, Jon and Kanna. To Simon for his great finds. To Laura and Diana for their patience with me. And to Tokyo for being a consistently fascinating place in which to live.

Acknowledgments

Cover photograph: Sensō-ji, Asakusa, Tokyo, Chris Stowers/Panos.

This Book

This 5th edition of Lonely Planet's *Pocket Tokyo* guidebook was researched and written by Rebecca Milner and Simon Richmond. The previous edition was also written by Rebecca Milner. This guidebook was produced by the following:

Destination Editor Laura Crawford **Product Editors** Kate Kiely, Alison Ridgway **Senior Cartographer** Diana Von Holdt **Book Designer** Jessica Rose **Assisting Editors** Rosie Nicholson, Charlotte Orr **Cover Researcher** Naomi Parker **Thanks to** Daniel Corbett, Anders Gronlund, Elizabeth Jones, Anne Mason, Wayne Murphy, Claire Naylor, Karyn Noble, Lauren Wellicome

Index

See also separate subindexes for:

⊗ **Eating p189**

⊕ **Drinking p190**

⊕ **Entertainment p190**

🔒 **Shopping p191**

Sights 000
Map Pages 000

Our Writers

Rebecca Milner

Rebecca came to Tokyo for 'just one year' in 2002 and still hasn't been able to tear herself away. She's lived west of Shinjuku and east of the Sumida and now shares an apartment in Shibuya (the quiet part) with her husband and cat. Her writing has appeared in the *Guardian*, *Japan Times*, CNN Travel and BBC Travel and Lonely Planet guides to Japan. When not on assignment, you can find her cycling around the city in search of new cafes, tracking down obscure onsen in the countryside or scuba diving in Okinawa.

Contributing Writer

Simon Richmond A travel writer, photographer and videographer, Simon won travel guidebook of the year for his first coauthored guidebook on Japan, published in 1999. He's also written several guidebooks to Tokyo (where he lived and worked as a journalist and editor in the early 1990s) and books on anime and manga. An author with Lonely Planet since 1999, Simon has worked for the company on many titles and features for its website. Read more about Simon's travels at www.simonrichmond.com and on Twitter and Instagram @simonrichmond.

Published by Lonely Planet Publications Pty Ltd
ABN 36 005 607 983
5th edition – August 2015
ISBN 978 1 74321 679 8
© Lonely Planet 2015 Photographs © as indicated 2015
10 9 8 7 6 5 4 3 2 1
Printed in China

Although the authors and Lonely Planet have taken all reasonable care in preparing this book, we make no warranty about the accuracy or completeness of its content and, to the maximum extent permitted, disclaim all liability arising from its use.